ROBOT

MEET THE MACHINES
OF THE FUTURE

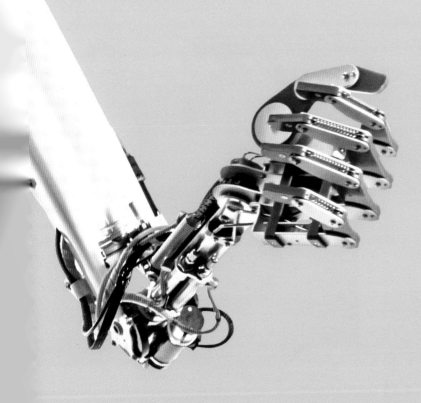

DK LONDON
Senior editor Steven Carton
Senior art editor Smiljka Surla
Picture researcher Nic Dean
Photographer Ruth Jenkinson
Jacket designers Smiljka Surla, Surabhi Wadhwa-Gandhi
Jacket editor Amelia Collins
Jacket design development manager Sophia MTT
Producer, pre-production Andy Hilliard
Senior producer Alex Bell
Managing editor Lisa Gillespie
Managing art editor Owen Peyton Jones
Publisher Andrew Macintyre
Associate publishing director Liz Wheeler
Art director Karen Self
Design director Phil Ormerod
Publishing director Jonathan Metcalf

DK DELHI
Senior editor Bharti Bedi
Senior art editor Shreya Anand
Editors Charvi Arora, Aadithyan Mohan
Art editor Revati Anand
Assistant art editors Baibhav Parida, Srishti Arora
Jacket designer Juhi Sheth
Jackets editorial coordinator Priyanka Sharma
Senior DTP designer Harish Aggarwal
DTP designers Nand Kishor Acharya,
Pawan Kumar, Vikram Singh
Managing jackets editor Saloni Singh
Pre-production manager Balwant Singh
Production manager Pankaj Sharma
Managing editor Kingshuk Ghoshal
Managing art editor Govind Mittal

Written by Laura Buller, Clive Gifford, Andrea Mills
Consultants Lucy Rogers, Michael Szollosy

First published in Great Britain in 2018 by
Dorling Kindersley Limited
80 Strand, London WC2R 0RL

Copyright © 2018 Dorling Kindersley Limited
A Penguin Random House Company
10 9 8 7 6 5 4 3 2
005–310748–Sept/2018

A CIP catalogue record for this book
is available from the British Library.
ISBN: 978-0-2413-4675-4

Printed and bound in Italy

A WORLD OF IDEAS:
SEE ALL THERE IS TO KNOW

www.dk.com

CON

T E N T S

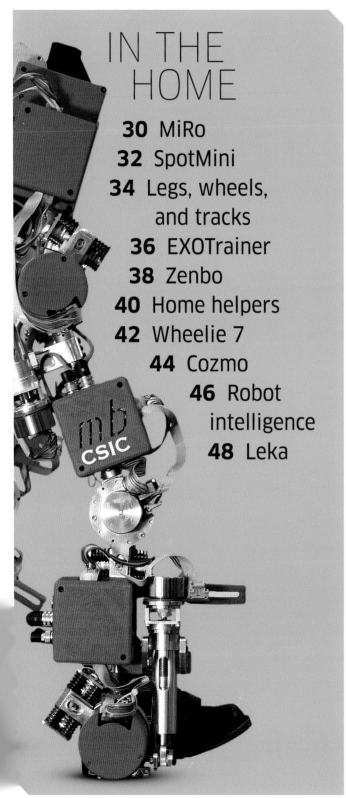

EVERYDAY BOTS

GOING TO EXTREMES

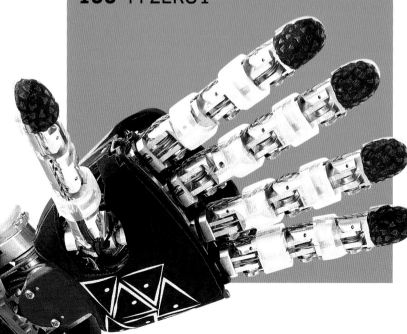

HERO BOTS

SPECIFICATION PANELS

Each robot profile features some or all of the specifications shown in this box.

ORIGIN
This indicates the country in which the robot was developed.

HEIGHT
The height of the robot

POWER
This indicates the source of power for the robot.

MANUFACTURER
This indicates the maker of the robot.

DEVELOPED/RELEASED
This indicates the year in which development work first began on the robot, or when the robot was commercially released.

WEIGHT
The weight of the robot

FEATURES
This includes the most characteristic and noteworthy features of the robot.

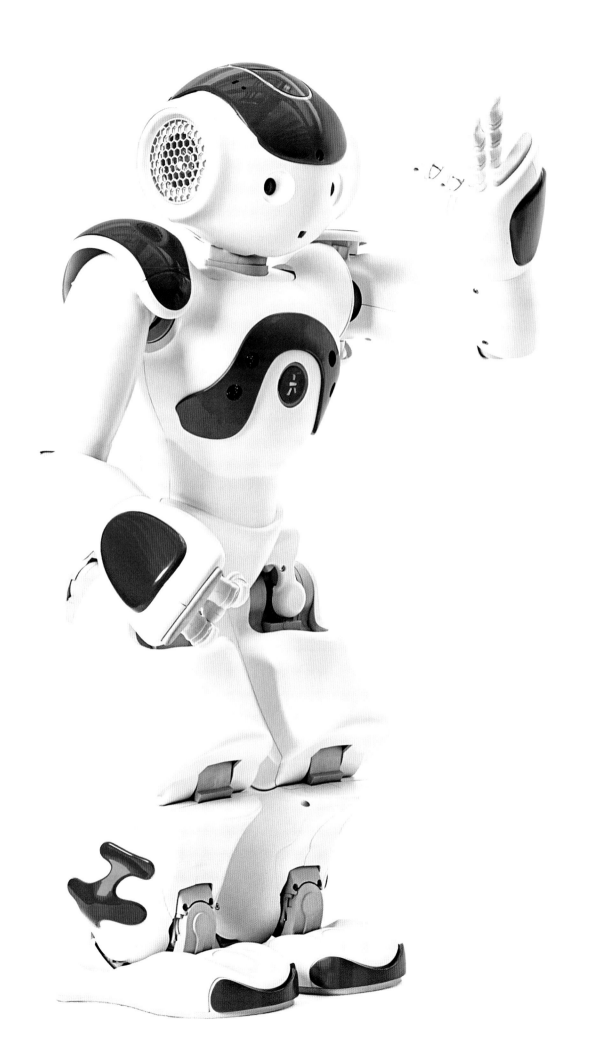

FOREWORD

When I was a child, robots were machines of the future, found only in books, comics, and films. I remember being a robot at a fancy dress party – I wore a cardboard box and a lot of tinfoil. But robots are no longer for the future – they are here and now and, for me, this is very exciting. Robots do not look how I imagined they would when I was a child - there is less tinfoil. They can also do things I hadn't imagined.

My favourite robot was a clockwork toy that waddled across the table. If you could make one, what would it look like? There are now so many to choose from. How does it move? Does it have wheels, tracks, or legs? Does it slither like a snake or swim like a fish? Does it fly? Can it see things we cannot see, smell things we cannot smell? Is it here among people or is it investigating areas we cannot go, like deep under the ocean or visiting other planets? What does your favourite robot do? Does it need a human to help it, or can it do everything for itself? Would you like to work with a robot? Would you like one as a pet? As a friend?

This book helps to bring many of jobs robots are doing for us now, to life. From exoskeletons that help people walk, to machines that make dangerous or dirty work safer for people. This book provides a comprehensive guide to the variety of today's robots – in size, complexity, and function. But it is not just a catalogue of robot types. It also gives a good understanding of how robots work, sense, move, and think.

Robots have come a long way since I was a child. But over the next few years they are going to improve further. They will become part of our everyday lives. To appreciate how they do the amazing things that they do, how they work, and how they are designed and controlled, is of great benefit – both now and in the future.

Lucy Rogers

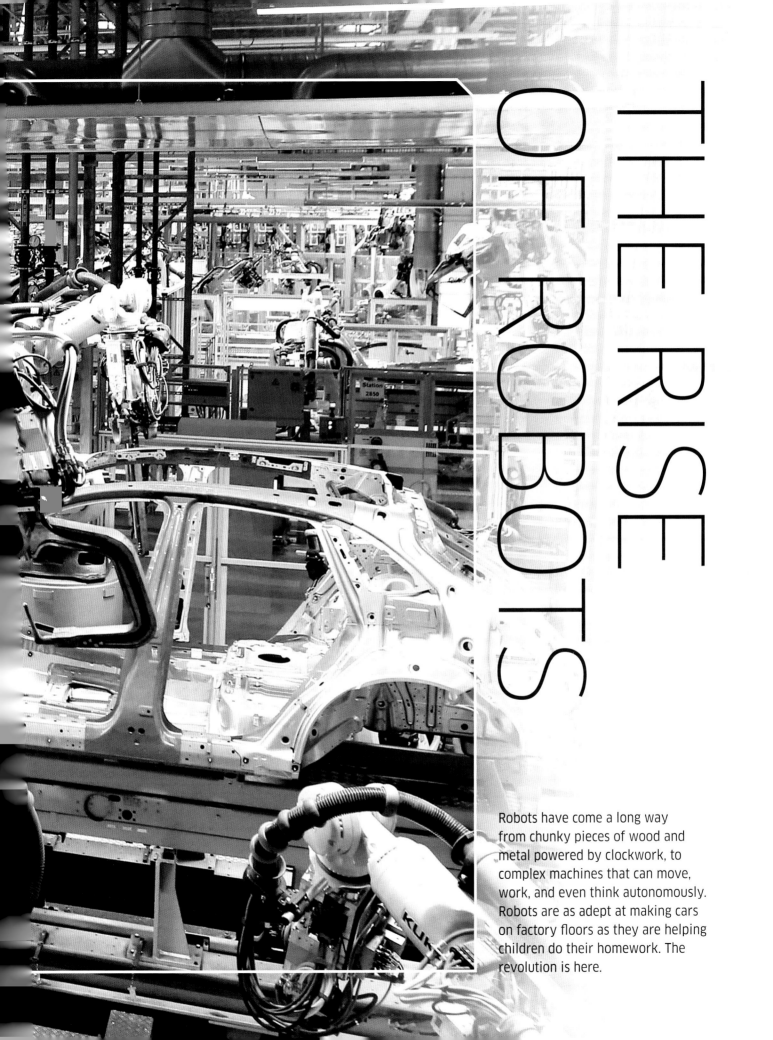

THE RISE OF ROBOTS

Robots have come a long way from chunky pieces of wood and metal powered by clockwork, to complex machines that can move, work, and even think autonomously. Robots are as adept at making cars on factory floors as they are helping children do their homework. The revolution is here.

WHAT IS A ROBOT?

What do you think of when you think about robots? Maybe you picture shiny humanoids with blinking lights and funny voices. Perhaps you think of a giant assembly line controlled by an all-robot crew. You might imagine robots as friendly companions, or even slightly menacing machines. Robots are simply computers that can sense, think, and move all on their own. They come in various sizes, shapes, and intelligence levels, and are designed for a wide range of tasks.

Though not integral to a robot's function, decorations such as this collar can be used to personalize a bot.

COLLAR

BOT BASICS
A social robot, such as MiRo, is a machine that is programmed by humans. MiRo's ability to sense, think, and move are controlled by an array of circuit boards.

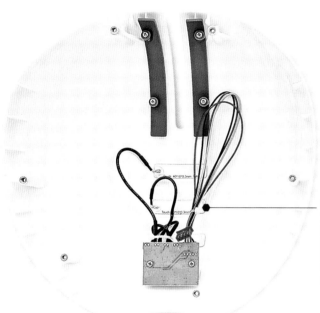

INSIDE BODY SHELL

Circuit boards control a robot's functions – from movement, to processors, and sensors.

BLUETOOTH MODULE

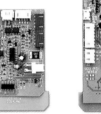

WHEEL DRIVE BOARD

FOREBRAIN BOARD

Touch sensor
This sensor allows a robot to be sensitive to human touch. MiRo will respond when you stroke its back.

NECK, LIFT, AND YAW MOTORS

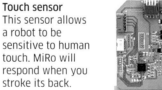

TAIL MOTOR CONTROL

SPINAL PROCESSOR

FRONT SENSOR ARRAY BOARD

THE FIRST ROBOTS
Robots aren't a modern invention. The first one may have been created around 400 BCE, when the ancient Greek mathematician Archytas built a steam-powered flying pigeon.

WHAT DO ROBOTS DO?
Robots can already do many of the things humans can, and they are only getting smarter and better. They can play, work, fix, build, and more.

WHY USE ROBOTS?
Robots are ideal for tasks that are too dangerous, dull, or dirty for humans to do. Robots do not get tired or bored, but must have clear instructions to do a task.

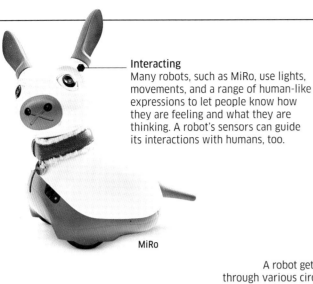

Interacting
Many robots, such as MiRo, use lights, movements, and a range of human-like expressions to let people know how they are feeling and what they are thinking. A robot's sensors can guide its interactions with humans, too.

MiRo

Sensing
Robots collect the information they need to make decisions via a range of devices called sensors. These pick up all sorts of information, including light and images, sound, touch, pressure, and location. MiRo's ears turn to detect the source of sound.

Thinking
A robot gets its brain power through various circuit boards. Each one performs a job by processing information and sending instructions for an outcome. Some robots need an internet connection to "think", while others are more or less able to make decisions on their own.

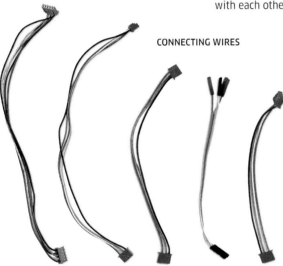

Connecting wires enable the parts of the robot to communicate with each other.

CONNECTING WIRES

INSIDE
MiRo's BODY

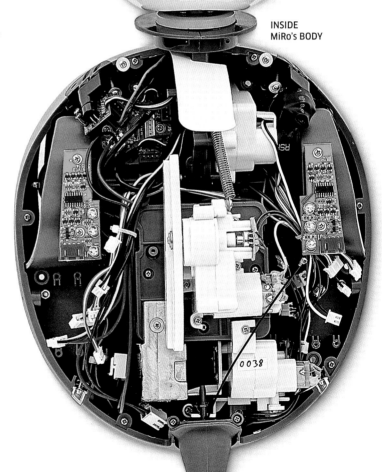

0038

FICTION TO FACT
Robots have inspired countless books and movies. In turn, the creative ideas of science-fiction (sci-fi) writers and moviemakers inspire many robot builders.

Moving
Most robots move about accurately, quickly, and smoothly on legs, wheels, or tracks. Moving body parts such as arms, heads, legs, and even wagging tails help bots communicate and do various jobs. Robots may even use pressurized air or water to move.

HOW ROBOTS WORK

Most robots are made up of the same basic components. A typical robot has a body to house its components, a way of moving, a sensory system to collect information from its environment, a way of interacting with objects, a source of electrical power, and a computer "brain" to control everything. Depending on the robot's task, these components can be put together in many different ways, which gives rise to the great diversity of robots that we can see in the world today.

BODY STRUCTURE

A robot's body must be strong enough to protect its internal parts, yet flexible enough to move. Aside from these concerns, robots are not limited in their shape. They can be as small as a single computer chip and larger than a house. Some, such as this slithering snakebot, are modelled on how particular animals move.

Robotic arms typically have the mechanical equivalent of a shoulder, an elbow, and a wrist.

FESTO

MOBILE BOTS

Some tasks require a robot to move about using tracks, wheels, or legs. Mobile bots like this camera-carrying GroundBot can explore dangerous places, such as earthquake zones or collapsed buildings, and power through tricky terrain like mud, snow, and rain.

SENSORY SYSTEM
Many robots, such as this therapy robot PARO, have sensors that collect data and tell the bot what is going on so that it can control its behaviour and respond appropriately. Some sensors are familiar ones, like cameras and motion and pressure devices. More complex sensors may use infrared, ultrasound, or lasers to collect information.

THE BRAINS BEHIND ROBOTS
A robot's central processing unit, its computer "brain", carries out instructions and moves the robot. Yet most robots can only do what they are programmed to do. The real brains behind robots are roboticists. These people design, build, and program bots, providing the right instructions they need to do their jobs. If that job changes, they can reprogram the robot.

The built-in pressure sensors can tell the robot's "brain" how hard it is holding something.

POWER UP!
A robot needs some sort of a power supply to drive its actuators – the mechanical devices that help it move. A robot might use batteries, or be plugged into a wall socket. It may even be powered by air or fluid pressure. NASA's Mars rovers use on-board solar cells to recharge their batteries.

The end effectors can even grasp delicate objects, such as a glass bottle, without damaging them.

HANDY HELPERS
Just as your arm moves your hand, a robot arm moves an end effector – a special tool such as a drill, surgical instrument, paint gun, or welding blowtorch. Different jobs require specific end effectors to carry out tasks such as grasping and carrying things.

ANCIENT AUTOMATA

For centuries, people have imagined and even created robot-like machines. Some were built simply to amaze and entertain – from flying wooden birds to life-sized roaring lions – while many were gifts to impress rulers. Other machines helped to tell the time or chart the stars. These incredible devices, known as automata, were not true robots, because they had no intelligence and could not be adapted to perform different jobs. But their invention did pave the way for the age of robots that followed.

ANTIKYTHERA MECHANISM

Look closer at this crusty old rock and you can spot gears with matching triangular teeth and a ring divided into degrees. This is the Antikythera mechanism, a fascinating device that may have enabled ancient Greeks to track the movement of the Sun, Moon, and the stars of the night sky. It can be thought of as a kind of early computer.

Archaeologists have recovered 82 fragments of the mechanism, buried on the seabed since around 80 BCE.

MYTHICAL MONSTERS

The ancient Greeks told tales of fantastic human-like mechanical creatures in their myths and legends. One such tale featured Talos, a giant bronze man forged by the blacksmith god Hephaestus. Talos guarded the coast of Crete to keep pirates and invaders away.

Talos stood 2.5 m (8 ft) tall in the story of the mythological hero Jason.

WATER CLOCK

Eight centuries ago, middle-eastern engineer Al-Jazari created many amazing contraptions. One of his best-known inventions was a water-powered elephant clock. He collected instructions for making his devices in *The Book of Knowledge of Ingenious Mechanical Devices*, written in 1206.

A ball is released every half hour to slide into the serpent's mouth.

The ball clangs into a cymbal and the elephant's driver beats his drums.

the sphere rotate.

ALEXANDRIAN MARVELS

The ancient Egyptian city of Alexandria became famous for its mechanical marvels from the 3rd to 1st centuries BCE. Engineers created water clocks topped with birds, drinking fountains for water or wine, and mechanical waiters. One of the star engineers was Hero of Alexandria, who built elaborate machines like this one. It is known as an aeolipyle, and featured a sphere that spun when the water inside it was heated.

PRAGUE ASTRONOMICAL CLOCK

By the 1400s, many great cathedrals or city centres featured animated clocks. At the stroke of each hour, the automata were set in motion. One of the most famous is the Prague Astronomical Clock, which is mounted on the old town hall in the Czech city, and is still working.

MECHANICAL MONK

In the 1560s, King Philip II of Spain commissioned a clockmaker named Juanelo Turriano to build a lifelike monk able to "walk" on its mechanical feet and move its eyes, lips, and head. Some 450 years later, the monk is still working.

The clockwork gears are hidden beneath the monk's cloak.

TEA SERVER

These Japanese puppet-robots are called Karakuri, and were made in the 1800s. They were used in theatres or wealthy people's homes to serve tea. When tea is poured in the cup on its tray, the robot moves to a guest, bows, and waits until the cup is taken before moving away.

ADVANCED AUTOMATA

By the 16th century, inventive creators were developing amazing mechanical machines with an uncanny ability to mimic people and animals. From metal ducks able to flap and quack, to an entire mechanical army, such fascinating creations captivated audiences across the globe. Many of these machines, known as "automata", were incredibly complex, and some of them are still in working order – including elaborate dolls that can write letters, sing songs, or even serve tea. People of the time were just as amazed by these marvellous machines as we are with super-modern robots today.

The Turk's mechanical arm was operated by a human inside the machine.

IT'S A HOAX!

In the 1770s, Hungarian inventor Wolfgang von Kempelen debuted his amazing creation – a mechanical man dressed in robes and a turban who could play chess against any challenger. "The Turk", however, was fake, operated by a person hidden underneath the chessboard.

The system of pulleys and weights was usually covered with robes.

The wind-up mechanism moves the robot.

MECHANICAL WRITER
Swiss inventor Pierre Jaquet-Droz created a trio of automatons in the late 1770s. His masterwork, a little boy sitting at a desk, could dip a pen into an inkwell and write up to 40 characters on paper.

Around 6,000 moving parts worked to operate the boy.

EUPHONIA
Created by Joseph Faber in the 1840s, this odd machine featured a doll-like head that was able to "speak" several languages through a system of bellows. Its operator used 17 keys to provide the sounds for various words. It could even sing.

ENIAC

Built between 1943 and 1945 to help the US Army with its ballistics calculations, ENIAC (Electronic Numerical Integrator And Computer) was the first large-scale computer. ENIAC's engineers claimed to have run more calculations in its first decade than the amount humans had performed from the start of time until ENIAC was built. An all-female team of programmers wrote the code that ENIAC used. On its 50th anniversary, the machine was recreated with modern circuits.

SPUTNIK 1

In October 1957, the former Soviet Union stunned the world with the launch of Sputnik I, the first artificial satellite. Although it was only about the size of a beach ball, Sputnik's impact was huge, as it spurred the Soviet Union's rival, the USA, into accelerating its own space program. The technological developments that resulted influenced robotics for years to come.

ANIMAL ROBOTS

Elmer and Elsie – the first moving robotic animals – were built by William Grey Walter in 1948. This pair of "tortoises" could move and change direction, and sense when another object was near. Touch- and light-sensitive contacts sent electrical signals to each robot's twin motors.

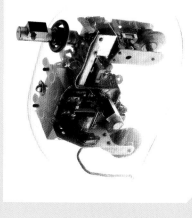

The see-through hole in the chest showed there was no human inside Elektro.

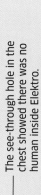

ELEKTRO AND SPARKO

Millions of people stood in line for hours to see Elektro, the 2.1-m- (7-ft-) tall metal man built for the 1939 New York World's Fair. A system of gears and electric motors enabled him to walk, move his arms, roll his head around, move and count his fingers, and open and close his mouth as he used his 700-word vocabulary. His robotic companion dog Sparko could beg, bark, and wag its tail.

Elektro was able to tell jokes, blow up balloons, and smoke, via its electrical relay system.

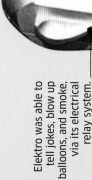

Jack Kilby's integrated circuit enabled computers and robots to be more efficient, smaller, and smarter.

TRANSISTORS

Electronic parts called transistors changed everything when they were invented in 1947, as they were tiny, long-lasting, and used less energy than previous technology. American electrical engineer Jack Kilby made a breakthrough in 1958 when he designed the integrated circuit – a tiny computer chip that made the invention of modern robots and small personal computers possible.

ROBOTIC ARMS

By 1961, robots were ready to get to work. The Unimate 1900 series became the first mass-produced robotic arm for factory automation. It made its television debut in 1966 when the American television audiences watched it knock a golf ball into a cup, pour drinks, and conduct a band on a show.

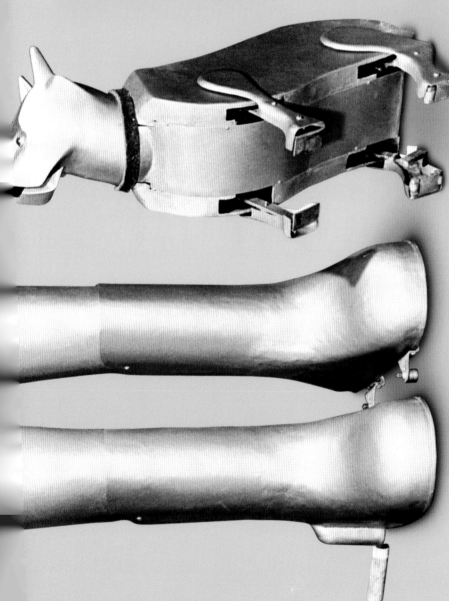

RISE OF REAL ROBOTICS

Rapid advances in electronics and technology in the 20th century set off a real robot revolution. Many scientists, inspired by science fiction (sci-fi), created ever more sophisticated robots. Smaller, cheaper, faster electronics enabled a rapid evolution, and the Space Race (between the USA and the former Soviet Union) provided an impetus to take technology to places it had never been. The quest for artificial intelligence remained a complex challenge, but robots were beginning to rise.

R.U.R.
Czech playwright Karel Capek used the word "robot" for a fictional humanoid in his 1920 play *R.U.R.* (*Rossum's Universal Robots*) – a tale about a company that created a soulless workforce of robots to replace humans.

METROPOLIS
The silent movie, *Metropolis* (1927), by Austrian-born director Fritz Lang, featured a robot called Maria. The robot was created by a mad scientist to help control the workers toiling away in the city of Metropolis.

ROBBY THE ROBOT
Loyal servant to the professor in the sci-fi classic film *Forbidden Planet* (1956), Robby can speak 188 languages, and has metal claws and a dome-head design that broke away from the usual "tin can" style of robots. Robby was really a 2.1-m- (7-ft-) tall suit worn by an actor. It was made of plastic, glass, metal, rubber, and Plexiglass.

ROBOTS IN CULTURE

Ask someone to describe a robot and chances are they'll talk about one of the mechanical marvels from books, theatre, television, or film. Indeed, the first mention of the word "robot" comes from a Czech theatre play from the 1920s called *R.U.R.*, and meant something akin to "forced labour". Robotic creations have surprised, amazed, and even terrified us, leaping to life from our stages, screens, and pages, but great science fiction (sci-fi) is not just entertainment. It has inspired developments in real scientific research for decades. Sci-fi also helps us understand the social and ethical implications of technology as we move to a future with robots.

TERMINATOR
Could robots take over the world, and wage total war against people? This is the premise of the *Terminator* (1984 onwards) films. Cyborg assassins called Terminators look like humans, but their goal is to destroy them. They travel back through time to target their victims. And if they don't succeed? They'll be back.

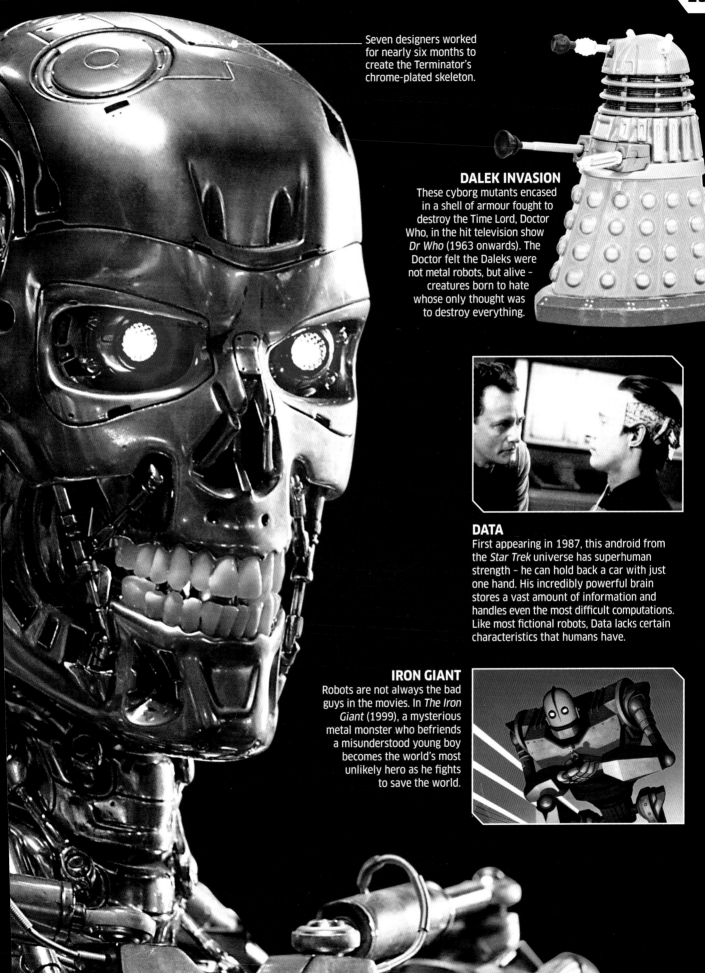

Seven designers worked for nearly six months to create the Terminator's chrome-plated skeleton.

DALEK INVASION

These cyborg mutants encased in a shell of armour fought to destroy the Time Lord, Doctor Who, in the hit television show *Dr Who* (1963 onwards). The Doctor felt the Daleks were not metal robots, but alive – creatures born to hate whose only thought was to destroy everything.

DATA

First appearing in 1987, this android from the *Star Trek* universe has superhuman strength – he can hold back a car with just one hand. His incredibly powerful brain stores a vast amount of information and handles even the most difficult computations. Like most fictional robots, Data lacks certain characteristics that humans have.

IRON GIANT

Robots are not always the bad guys in the movies. In *The Iron Giant* (1999), a mysterious metal monster who befriends a misunderstood young boy becomes the world's most unlikely hero as he fights to save the world.

This bot reacts to the user's movements with a glowing symbol on its shiny black screen.

MODERN ROBOTS

For so long, TV and film were filled with stories about how the robots were coming, but they really started to arrive in the early 21st century. They may not look like the humanoid robots from sci-fi, but they have made their way into many different areas of our lives. From robot pets to delivery drones, and from assistant bots to robotic exoskeletons, robots are very much a part of the modern world.

SOCIAL BOTS

Voice assistant robots, such as Jibo, can look, listen, and learn, and are happy to help with your day. These domestic bots might just become as common as an electric kettle. From controlling all the other gadgets in your home, to reading you the news and weather reports, they can be useful companions.

BEST FRIENDS

Companion bots, such as Sony's robotic dog aibo, belong to a new class of machines that are intelligent and useful. They can help disabled people with daily tasks, engage with children who have special needs, or remind elderly people to take their medicines.

A total of 22 moveable parts give aibo a lifelike range of movements, including a wagging tail.

EYE IN THE SKY

Whether you call them UAVs (unmanned aerial vehicles) or just flying robots, drones are filling our skies. From hexacopters (above) loaded with video cameras to scan a disaster area or a remote military base, to drones making deliveries, these robots can quickly and efficiently reach places that people cannot.

SMART CARS

Computers have revolutionized almost every aspect of cars, to the point where some can even be considered true robots. This is because the very latest, such as the Rimac C_Two, offer some level of autonomy – essentially being able to drive themselves if required. The case for driverless smart cars is clear – they will not get tired or forget instructions, but many people are unsure whether the technology is safe enough just yet.

The safety frame helps children keep their balance as they move.

The OLED (organic light-emitting diode) panels in its eyes glow to help the bot display expressions.

WEARABLE BOTS

The ATLAS 2030 is a lower body exoskeleton bot that helps children with neuromuscular diseases walk. Its parts mimic the functions of actual muscles. Wearable robots like this one can not only help those with a physical disability or recovering from an injury, but can also enhance anyone's physical performance.

TYPES OF ROBOT

Robots come in all shapes and sizes, and are usually grouped together by the tasks they do – from working in fields to assisting surgeons. The robots featured in this book fall into ten categories, but many of these multi-tasking robots can be grouped in more than one.

WORK ROBOTS

Robots are being increasingly used to carry out tasks that may be dangerous, repetitive, or boring for humans. Rugged terrain, tight spaces, or bad weather do not deter these work robots. These robots work independently, guided by sensors and cameras. The most common type of work robot is a robotic arm – capable of a variety of tasks, including welding, painting, and assembly.

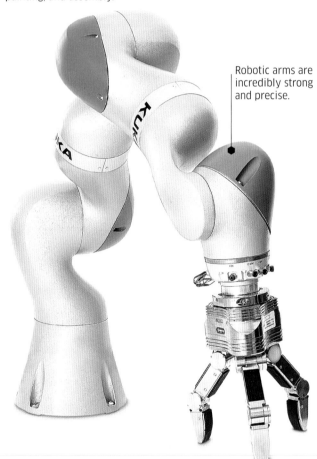

Robotic arms are incredibly strong and precise.

SOCIAL ROBOTS

Designed to interact with humans, social robots are programmed to understand human interactions and be able to respond. These friendly bots can be your companions, teachers, or just be around to assist or entertain. Some social robots are designed to be used by people with medical conditions such as autism or learning difficulties.

Leka is a multi-function robotic ball that helps children with learning difficulties.

The Mars 2020 rover will conduct science experiments on the Red Planet.

SPACE ROBOTS

It is safer and cheaper to send robotic explorers to find out more about the objects in the Solar System than to send humans. Space-exploration robots are built to withstand the harsh conditions of the worlds beyond Earth. While some probes fly close to these bodies, many craft land and send data and images back to scientists on Earth.

COLLABORATIVE ROBOTS

Industrial robots that work safely alongside people are known as collaborative robots, or cobots. Human co-workers can train these cobots using a tablet or by physically moving them to show how a task is done. Once programmed, collaborative robots work in the same space as humans, usually taking on repetitive or precise jobs, such as packing boxes or assembling electronic parts.

YuMi's powered arms have a wide range of movement.

ABB

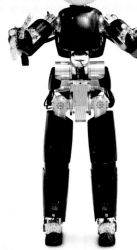

iCub is an artificially intelligent bot that can learn from its interactions with humans.

HUMANOID ROBOTS

Humanoid robots are created to resemble the human form, and have a head and face, and usually limbs. Some are able to walk on two legs, while others roll on wheels or tracks. Humanoid robots tend to have a more developed artificial intelligence (AI) compared to other robots, and some are even able to form memories or think for themselves.

BIOMIMETIC ROBOTS

The natural world of plants and animals has provided the inspiration for many robots. These bots are called "biomimetic" as they imitate some form of natural life. They not only look like their real-life inspirations, but can also imitate their extraordinary feats as well, including jumping, flying, and swimming. The lessons learned from building these robots help roboticists in a wide range of technologies.

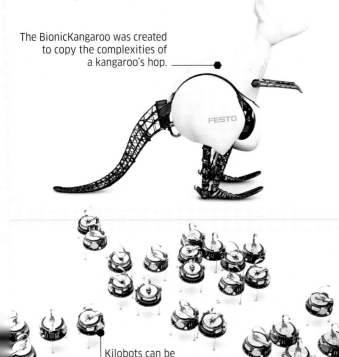

The BionicKangaroo was created to copy the complexities of a kangaroo's hop.

Kilobots can be programmed in large numbers simultaneously.

SWARM ROBOTS

Hundreds of simple robots come together to form a swarm that functions as one big, intelligent robot. Inspired by social insects in nature, these robots can complete some tasks more easily than one robot working alone. Individual robots communicate with each other to coordinate their movements.

PILOTED ROBOTS

Not all robots are fully autonomous. Many can be controlled remotely by a human pilot, while some others may receive direct instructions from humans. Some giant robots can even be driven by a human, who sits in a cockpit and pilots the robot from within.

Chimp is a rescue robot that can help humans in distress.

HOME-HELP ROBOTS

Home-help robots help with everyday chores, such as cleaning, carrying shopping, and even cooking meals. Some also act like personal assistants, helping us to organize our time or to find information online. In future, robots will be able to take on more and more jobs around the home.

Zenbo can play with children, help adults with various tasks, and even secure the home when everybody is out.

MEDICAL ASSISTANT ROBOTS

Robotic technology is gaining prominence in the field of medicine and healthcare. Scientists have developed robots that help people with disabilities – from artificial limbs and robotic wheelchairs, to exoskeletons that help people walk or lift objects.

EXOTrainer was designed to help children with spinal muscular atrophy.

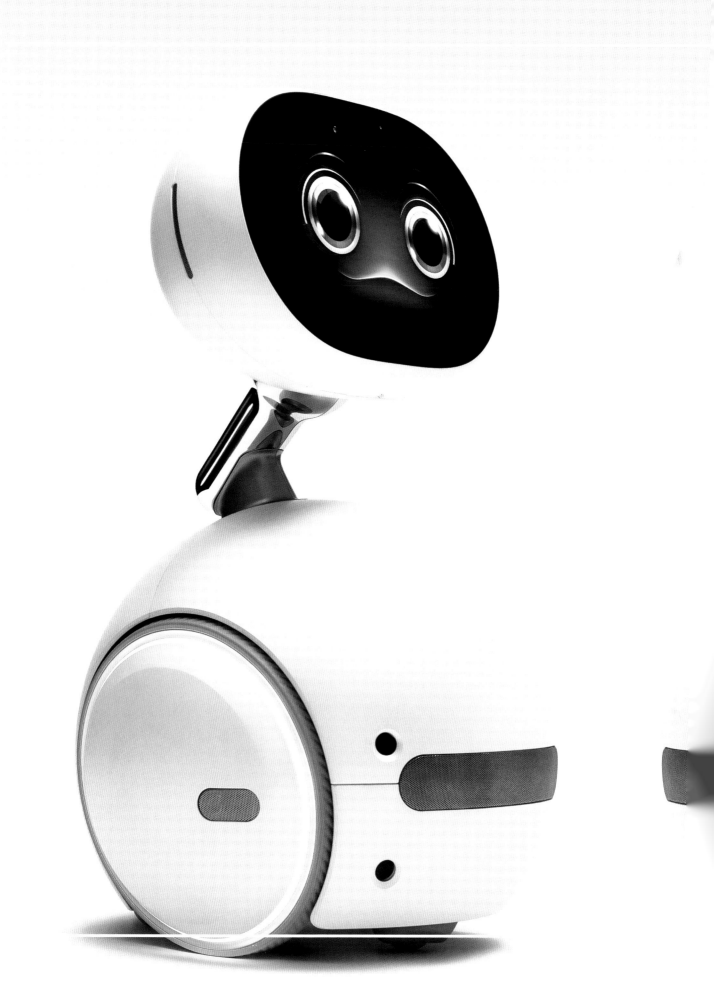

IN THE HOME

Home is where the heart is, but it's also where more and more robots are finding a way of helping humans. These friendly robots can entertain us, clean our homes, help humans with disabilities, or just be our friends.

MANUFACTURER
Consequential Robotics and
the University of Sheffield

ORIGIN
UK

DEVELOPED
2016

WEIGHT
5 kg (11 lb)

POWER
Battery

HOW IT WORKS

MiRo is a biomimetic robot, which means it imitates the characteristics of animals found in nature. The sensors packed in MiRo allow it to react to different stimuli – such as sound, touch, and light.

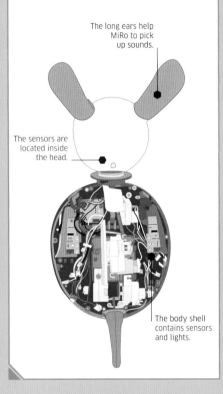

The long ears help MiRo to pick up sounds.

The sensors are located inside the head.

The body shell contains sensors and lights.

❝The animal kingdom holds the key to the **future of robotics.❞**

Manufacturers, **MiRo**

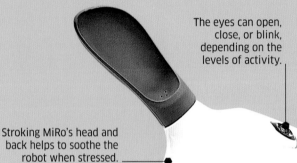

The eyes can open, close, or blink, depending on the levels of activity.

Stroking MiRo's head and back helps to soothe the robot when stressed.

MiRo can be accessorized by colourful collars and neck scarves.

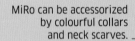

The nose houses a sonar sensor. This helps the robot to move without falling or colliding with objects in its environment.

SUPER SENSES

Like many animals, MiRo has strong senses. Its big eyes provide 3D light-sensitive vision, while the long rotating ears have stereo microphones to pick up sounds. Miniature sensors help the bot to respond to the slightest stroke or pat.

FEATURES
Range of sensors, cameras,
and microphones

The ears raise and
rotate to follow the
direction of sounds.

LIGHT SENSITIVE

MiRo's light sensors can detect the difference between light and dark,
and recognize when it is day or night. The robot has LED light displays
to represent a variety of "emotions", which can be learned and understood
by MiRo's owner.

Green light
expresses
excitement,
happiness,
or calm.

Red light
means stress.

EXCITED MiRo

STRESSED MiRo

A group of MiRos
respond to each other by
watching and moving
closer to one another.

MiRo uses its body
language to show
its "emotions".

SOCIAL ROBOT
MiRo

Expert studies of animal brains and behaviour have
resulted in MiRo – a fully programmable bot, with
the charms of a real animal but none of the challenges.
MiRo is aimed at children and elderly people who would
enjoy all the benefits of a close relationship with a robotic
best friend without the responsibilities of walking, feeding,
and cleaning it. This one-stop cuddle-shop responds to
love and affection like a real pet, giving owners a reliable,
robust, and fun companion.

A cocked head suggests
MiRo is interested.

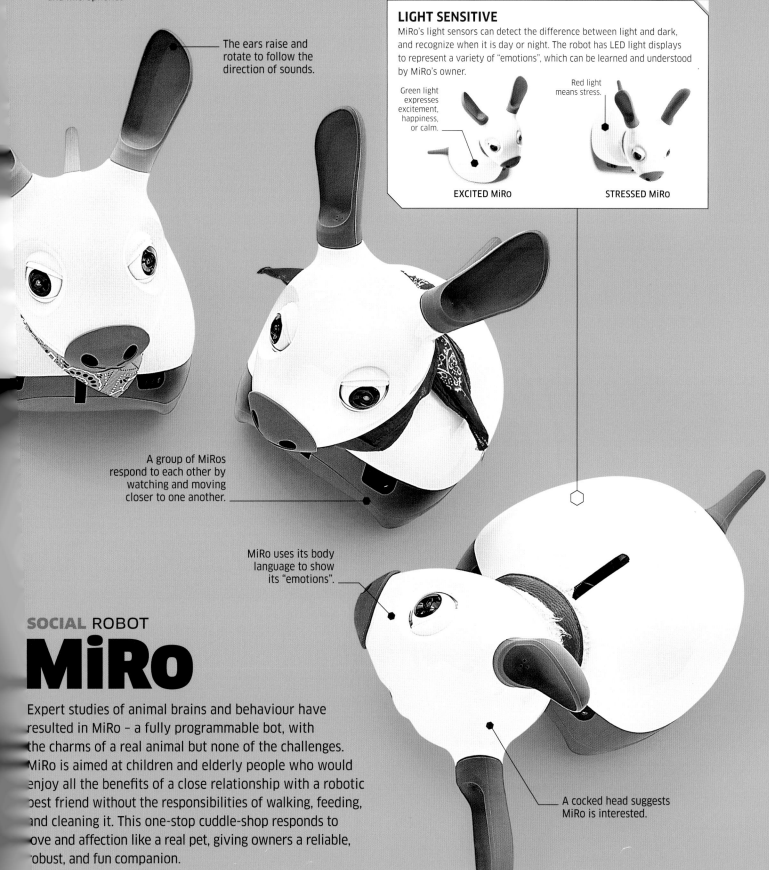

MANUFACTURER
Boston Dynamics

ORIGIN
USA

DEVELOPED
2017

HEIGHT
84 cm (33 in)

WEIGHT
30 kg (66 lb)

AROUND THE HOME

In future, it is hoped that SpotMini can help disabled people get around at home and in work. Boston Dynamics have released videos showing SpotMini using a special arm attachment to open a heavy door.

SpotMini uses arm attachments to grip door handle

SpotMini pulls back door, using a foot to stop it from shutting

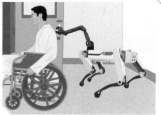
Door is held open to allow wheelchair user through

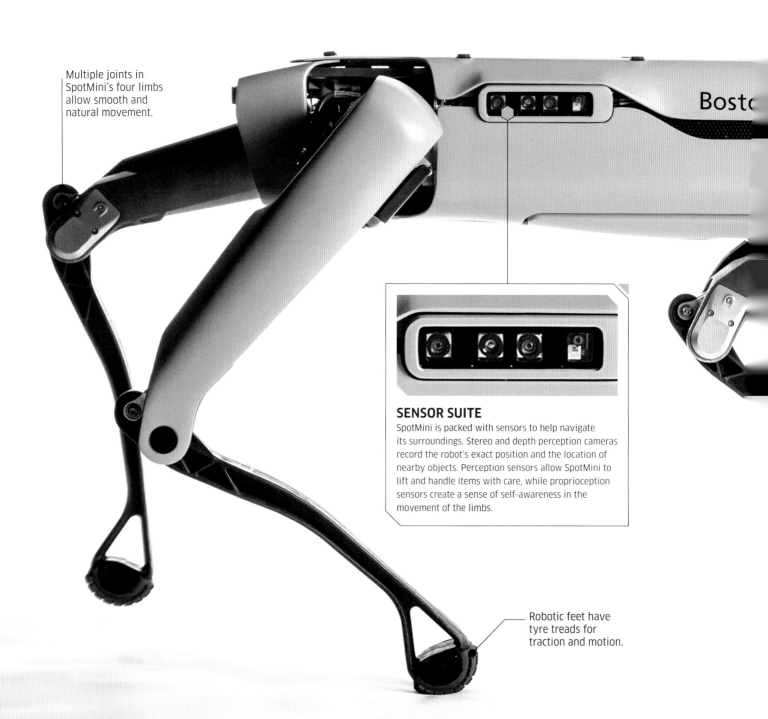

Multiple joints in SpotMini's four limbs allow smooth and natural movement.

SENSOR SUITE

SpotMini is packed with sensors to help navigate its surroundings. Stereo and depth perception cameras record the robot's exact position and the location of nearby objects. Perception sensors allow SpotMini to lift and handle items with care, while proprioception sensors create a sense of self-awareness in the movement of the limbs.

Robotic feet have tyre treads for traction and motion.

HOME-HELP ROBOT
SpotMini

With the potential to become man's best friend, SpotMini is a four-legged helper bot based on a real dog. This clever canine goes way beyond chasing and fetching, though. The small and sleek SpotMini has masterminded picking up objects, climbing stairs, and navigating obstacles. Test runs showed it opening doors with ease, thanks to a manoeuvrable arm extending from the body. SpotMini runs on electricity for 90 minutes without charging, perhaps making it the most energetic robotic pet pooch out there.

Yellow plastic exterior is highly robust and durable.

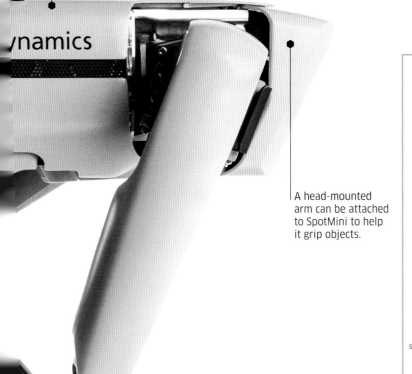

A head-mounted arm can be attached to SpotMini to help it grip objects.

SPOT

Spot is another four-legged robot developed by Boston Dynamics. Built for moving on rough terrain, Spot uses its sensors and stereo vision for navigation and maintaining its balance when moving. It can run for 45 minutes on a single battery charge and can carry up to 23 kg (50 lb) of load.

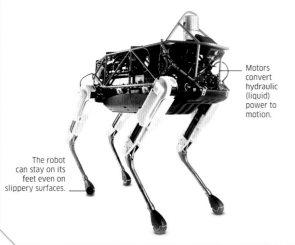

Motors convert hydraulic (liquid) power to motion.

The robot can stay on its feet even on slippery surfaces.

"These robots explore the possibilities, and try to expand the capabilities, of robots."

Marc Raibert, CEO, **Boston Dynamics**

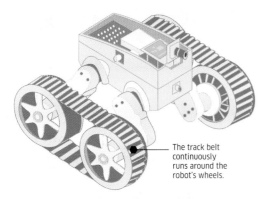

The track belt continuously runs around the robot's wheels.

Tracked robot

Tracks, similar to those found on tanks and bulldozers, tend to offer slower movement than wheels, as a lot of the robot is in contact with the ground. But they excel at providing grip for tackling slopes and crossing rough, unpredictable terrain. Most tracked robots steer by reversing the direction of one of the tracks, which causes the robot to skid around as it moves.

LEGS, WHEELS, AND TRACKS

Humans move almost without thinking, but a robot's movement, often known as locomotion, has to be carefully designed and programmed. Stability, balance, and the ability to overcome obstacles are important issues that have to be addressed. For robots on land, the three most common locomotion systems use legs, wheels, and tracks. Within these three broad types, there are lots of options available for robotics engineers to think about.

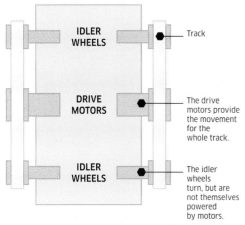

IDLER WHEELS — Track

DRIVE MOTORS — The drive motors provide the movement for the whole track.

IDLER WHEELS — The idler wheels turn, but are not themselves powered by motors.

MOVING FORWARDS

MOVING BACKWARDS

To turn in either direction, one track moves forwards and the other backwards.

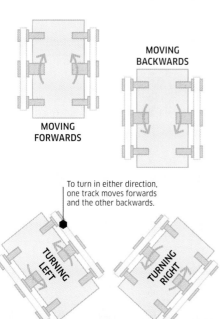

TURNING LEFT

TURNING RIGHT

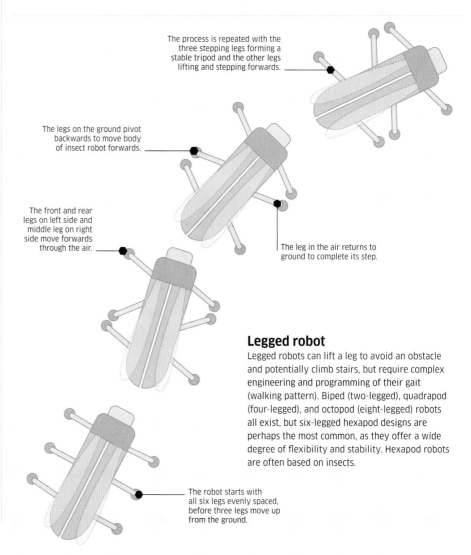

The process is repeated with the three stepping legs forming a stable tripod and the other legs lifting and stepping forwards.

The legs on the ground pivot backwards to move body of insect robot forwards.

The front and rear legs on left side and middle leg on right side move forwards through the air.

The leg in the air returns to ground to complete its step.

Legged robot

Legged robots can lift a leg to avoid an obstacle and potentially climb stairs, but require complex engineering and programming of their gait (walking pattern). Biped (two-legged), quadrapod (four-legged), and octopod (eight-legged) robots all exist, but six-legged hexapod designs are perhaps the most common, as they offer a wide degree of flexibility and stability. Hexapod robots are often based on insects.

The robot starts with all six legs evenly spaced, before three legs move up from the ground.

Wheeled robot

Wheels tend to offer the fastest, simplest, and most efficient method of locomotion for mobile land bots. As less of the wheel is in contact with the ground at any one time, there is a reduction in the slowing force of friction acting upon each wheel. As a result, it is easier for the motors to turn some or all of a robot's wheels. Wheeled robots prefer travelling over smooth ground; they can struggle with a rock-strewn surface. Some planetary rovers overcome this problem by mounting their wheels on a rocker-bogie hinging suspension system. These can lift and tilt the body as the wheels ride up and over an obstacle. Designers and engineers plan the wheel layout around what the robot will be used for.

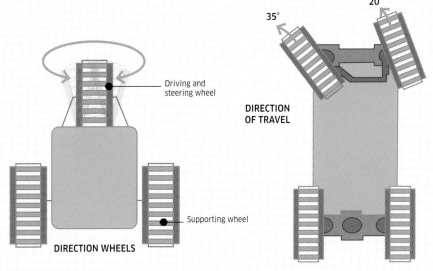

Driving and steering wheel

Supporting wheel

DIRECTION WHEELS

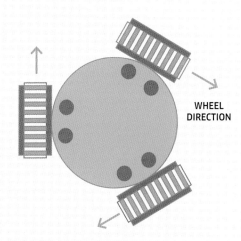

20°

35°

DIRECTION OF TRAVEL

DIRECTION OF TRAVEL

WHEEL DIRECTION

Tricycle drive robots

This layout features two supporting back wheels that give the robot a stable base. The single front wheel both powers the robot forwards and can pivot left or right to steer the robot and make it turn. This design is simple, but does not offer as many ways of turning as other designs.

Four-wheeled robots

Most four-wheeled robots use Ackerman steering. This involves the rear wheels propelling the robot forwards, while the front wheels turn to steer. When turning, the inner wheel (left) turns at a greater angle than the outer wheel, which reduces the chances of skidding.

Three-wheeled omnibots

In this design, the wheels themselves do not turn to steer the robot. To move in one direction, signals are sent from the robots' controller to move the wheels at different speeds. This layout means the robot can turn about its own axis when each wheel is turned at the same speed.

Balancing

A human's balance is controlled by the brain, the inner ear, and more than 600 muscles. In contrast, robots use devices such as tilt and joint angle sensors to monitor where their parts are and whether they're in danger of toppling over. Many robots with six or more legs keep half of them on the ground to maintain a stable base, while the other legs move. The problem for two-legged robots is that lifting one leg makes them unstable and requires vast amounts of computing power, coding, and sensors to compensate. The same is the case with single and two-wheeled robots which need constant small adjustments to stay balanced.

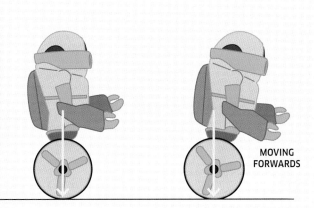

MOVING FORWARDS

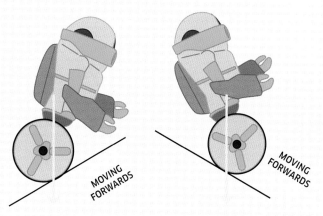

MOVING FORWARDS

MOVING FORWARDS

Moving ahead

When still, a two wheeled robot's centre of gravity is positioned squarely over the middle of its wheels to keep it upright. To move ahead, the robot leans forwards in order to counteract the forces seeking to push the robot backwards as its wheels turn forwards.

On a slope

A robot leans forwards into a slope as it climbs upwards. This keeps the robot's body weight and centre of gravity directly over the part of the wheel making contact with the ground. The opposite is true when the robot descends on a downward slope.

MANUFACTURER
Spanish National
Research Council (CSIC)
and Marsi Bionics

ORIGIN
Spain

DEVELOPED
2016

WEIGHT
12 kg
(26.5 lb)

MEDICAL ASSISTANT ROBOT

EXOTrainer

Robotics technologies are helping millions of people with limited mobility, many of whom are children. Robotic exoskeletons are structures that sit outside the body and help support and move it. EXOTrainer is one such device that helps wearers to stand and walk. It is designed to aid children between the ages of three and 14 who suffer from spinal muscular atrophy (SMA), a genetic disease that makes muscles weaker and affects the children's ability to move. EXOTrainer's smart joint system adjusts to the wearer, and can alter its own joints' stiffness and angle of movement as it mimics human muscles during walking.

HOW IT WORKS

Every step taken with the EXOTrainer requires a complex series of movements involving joints on both legs of the exoskeleton. The EXOTrainer automatically adjusts the stiffness of all of its joints to allow for the hardness of the walking surface. As the foot reaches the ground, the ankle and knee joints react to cushion the impact.

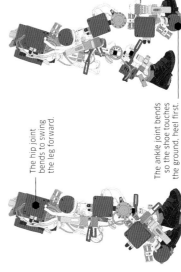

The hip joint bends to swing the leg forward.

The ankle joint bends so the shoe touches the ground, heel first.

After motors swing the bent leg past the standing leg, the knee joint straightens the lower leg as the step is taken.

The five motors in each leg whirr into action as they move the joints that bend the hip and knee to lift a foot off the floor.

FOR ADULTS

The ReWalk 6.0 exoskeleton for adults is lightweight, and powered by a battery supported by the hips. When it senses a tilt forward in the user's body angle, it starts to take steps by using its motors positioned at the hip and knee. It can achieve speeds of 2.6 km/h (1.6 mph).

The on-board computer instructs the motors to coordinate their movement into a natural walking action.

The frame is made of titanium and aluminium. The parts are telescopic, which means they can be made longer or shorter to fit the user.

ATLAS 2030

EXOTrainer is modelled on an existing exoskeleton – ATLAS 2030. This device can be used with children who are at least 95 cm (37.4 in) tall. The exoskeleton can be adjusted in size so that a growing child can continue to use the device.

The adjustable straps fit around the user's legs to hold them snugly.

The knee joint discs are powered by an electric motor and turn as the legs are lifted up off the floor.

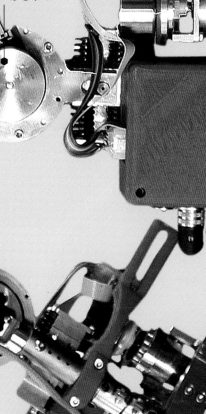

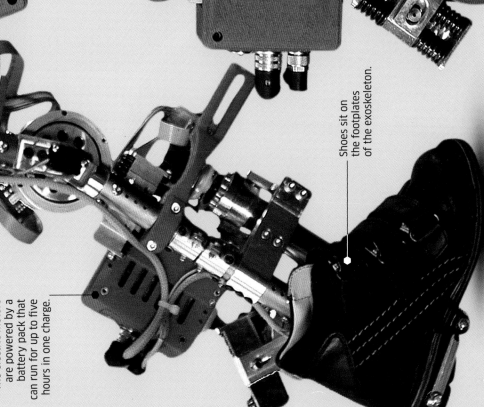

Shoes sit on the footplates of the exoskeleton.

The electric motors are powered by a battery pack that can run for up to five hours in one charge.

MANUFACTURER
Asus

ORIGIN
Taiwan

DEVELOPED
2016

HEIGHT
62 cm
(24.5 in)

REMOTE READY

With the Zenbo app, users can remotely control other smart household devices. These include security systems, lights, televisions, locks, and heating and cooling systems. In case of a medical emergency, Zenbo can even send photos and a voice or video alert to the app to get help.

HOME-HELP ROBOT
ZENBO

This friendly home-bot is designed to become a happy member of your family. Zenbo's developers set out to create a robot that's right for everyone – whether they are comfortable with technology or not. Zenbo can move on its own, communicate, and understand speech. The bot is capable of looking after the home whether its inhabitants are in or out. It can be a playmate for kids, a helping hand for adults, and a valuable and watchful companion for the elderly.

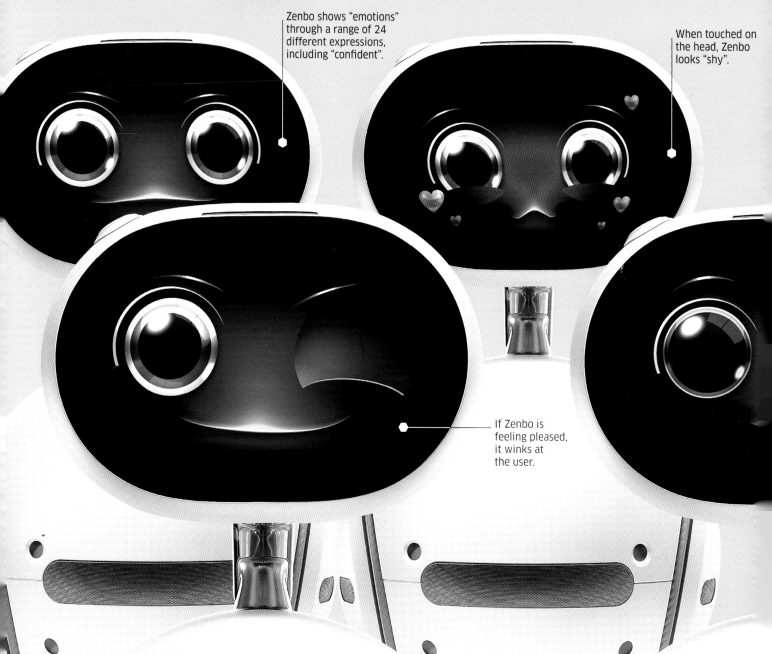

Zenbo shows "emotions" through a range of 24 different expressions, including "confident".

When touched on the head, Zenbo looks "shy".

If Zenbo is feeling pleased, it winks at the user.

WEIGHT
10 kg
(22 lb)

POWER
Battery

FEATURES
Learns and
adapts according
to user preference

39

TOUCH CONTROL

In addition to displaying the robot's expression, Zenbo's 25.6-cm (10.1-in) multi-touch panel can also stream movies, handle video calls, and even display recipes. The display is designed to bridge the digital gap for older users, who can shop, make calls, and use social media with simple voice commands.

The head has a camera and 3D depth camera, plus light sensor.

One of four drop sensors, which detects stairs and other hazards.

Wheel LED lights indicate how much power Zenbo has left, and if it is doing a task.

Sonar sensor helps Zenbo navigate its environment.

FULL VIEW

A USB port makes Zenbo ready for data and updates.

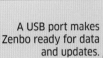

Zenbo's default expression

Zenbo shows when it's "happy".

Users can combine different expressions to create a unique personality for Zenbo.

▲ Kobi picks up leaves before they pile up.

GARDEN BOT

A green-fingered gizmo that can cut the grass and collect the leaves, **Kobi** leaves you with an immaculate lawn. Its GPS system and sensors prevent any collisions on the job. By following local weather forecasts, this gardening bot warns when wintry weather is on the way. Attach snow tyres and watch Kobi blow snow up to 12 m (40 ft) away.

▼ The battery-powered Kobi has silent motors, security features, and a top speed of 5 km/h (3 mph).

HOME HELPERS

Nobody really likes having to do the sweeping or mopping at home, but robots can't get enough of it! These bots take the drudgery out of everyday activities by remembering your preferences and taking it from there. Ever-ready to do the chores, they don't cut corners and never get tired.

▲ The water is manually added to the robot to be sprayed from its nozzle.

MOP BOT

When this teeny-tiny robot takes to the floor, it cleans up completely. The battery-powered **Braava jet** robotic mop can wet mop, damp sweep, or dry sweep. Using two wheels for motion, it repeats a cycle of squirting water, scrubbing floors, and mopping down afterwards in areas up to 25 sq m (270 sq ft). The super small size means it squeezes into even the tightest corners.

Pressing the "CLEAN" button wakes the robot, and pressing it again makes the bot start cleaning.

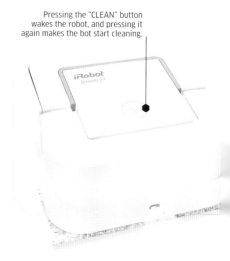

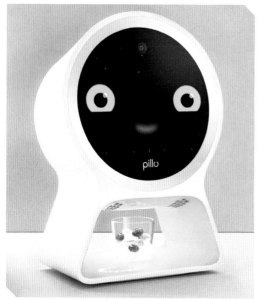

STAYING HEALTHY

A home health robot, **Pillo** is prepared to answer your questions and dispense medication when you need it. Using facial recognition software to distinguish between faces, Pillo learns and remembers each individual's healthcare needs. In a serious situation, it can connect to medical professionals for further advice and assistance.

◄ HD cameras, and internal sensors inside Pillo help in personal healthcare management.

DUST DEVIL

The ultimate dust hunter, **Roomba 900** series uses advanced navigation systems, visual localization, and a sensor suite to cross carpets and traverse tiles as it sucks up and brushes away anything in its path. Happy to do the dirty work, Roomba 900 recharges and continues automatically until your home is spotless.

The light-touch bumper helps the bot sense walls.

The "CLEAN" button starts and ends a cleaning cycle.

▲ The robot home app allows you to start a clean immediately or schedule a timely clean before you return home.

▲ Roomba 900 builds a map of the rooms in your house to intelligently navigate its surroundings.

▶ This stylish, sleek robot has a low-lying design so it can thoroughly clean under furniture.

The camera maps each room.

POOL PAL

Swimming pools are perfect for a splash, but cleaning them is far from fun. Drop **Mirra** in at the deep end and the cleaning cycle gets under way without you getting your hands wet. An in-built vacuum, pump, and filter system ensure this bot keeps the water and swimming pool squeaky clean with the minimum of fuss. Mirra circulates more than 18,000 litres (4,000 gallons) of water an hour, removing anything from large debris such as leaves and bugs, to small particles like algae and bacteria.

▲ The wheels power Mirra as its spinning scrub brush takes away debris from the pool floor.

▲ Once the job is done, the basket is taken out and the contents removed, so Mirra is ready for the next clean.

MANUFACTURER
HOOBOX Robotics

ORIGIN
Brazil

RELEASED
2016

HOW IT WORKS

To control the wheelchair, the user can select one of five facial expressions, each one moving the wheelchair in a specific way – backwards, forwards, left, right, and stopping its movement. When the software detects one of these expressions from the camera images, it sends signals to Gimme, a robotic gripper fitted over the wheelchair's joystick, which then moves the wheelchair.

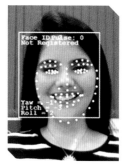
FULL SMILE

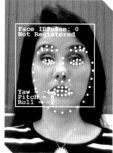
EYEBROWS UP

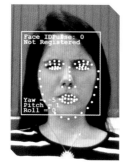
EYEBROWS DOWN

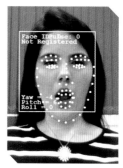
CHIN DOWN

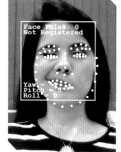
HALF SMILE

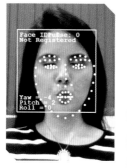
KISS

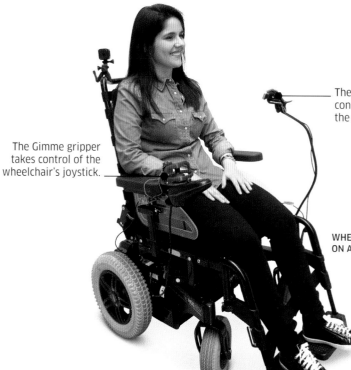

The Gimme gripper takes control of the wheelchair's joystick.

The camera continually scans the user's face.

WHEELIE 7 KIT ON A WHEELCHAIR

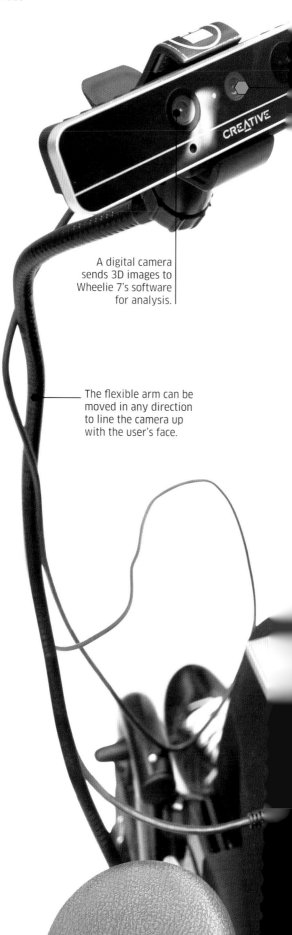

A digital camera sends 3D images to Wheelie 7's software for analysis.

The flexible arm can be moved in any direction to line the camera up with the user's face.

DETECTING EXPRESSIONS

Wheelie 7's software analyses 78 different points on a person's face. By judging changes in distance between each of the points, the software can detect nine different facial expressions, including "full smile", "kiss", and "tongue out".

Eight points are analysed on each eyebrow.

MEDICAL ASSISTANT ROBOT

WHEELIE 7

Imagine controlling a machine by raising your eyebrows or sticking your tongue out. Well, the Wheelie 7 robotic assistant does precisely that. Designed to aid people who have limited mobility, the device recognizes facial expressions captured by a special digital camera and converts them into commands to move a motorized wheelchair. The "7" in the name is a reference to how easy it is to set up – it takes just seven minutes to install on a regular wheelchair.

Facial recognition software analyses camera images to detect expressions.

MANUFACTURER
Anki

ORIGIN
USA

SOCIAL ROBOT

COZMO

Cozmo is small in stature, big on brains, and always up for fun. This free spirit will roam around looking for adventure. Competitive Cozmo comes packed with games, so expect a victory dance when it beats you! Watch out, though. This bad loser goes into an incredible sulk if it is not the winner. When Cozmo is tired, it sleeps in its charging dock where you'll hear it snoring away. But don't dismiss it as another toy: Cozmo is intelligent enough to be able to recognize and react to people's facial expressions.

Cozmo's robotic arms work like levers to lift or drop its cubes.

Interactive cubes are used to play a variety of games with Cozmo.

A front camera, AI vision system, and facial recognition software allow Cozmo to constantly scan its environment and recognize people.

COZMO STACKING CUBES

CHANGING FACES

This robot's "emotions" are controlled by an in-built "emotion engine". The high-definition screen changes the shape and size of Cozmo's bright blue eyes to register a huge variety of feelings. Facial recognition technology allows Cozmo to scan its surroundings and light up when it sees a familiar face.

NEUTRAL

HAPPY

SAD

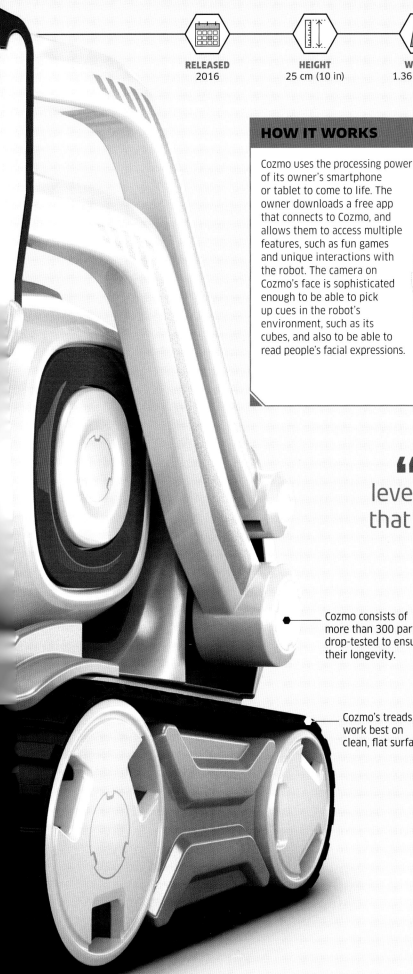

RELEASED 2016	**HEIGHT** 25 cm (10 in)	**WEIGHT** 1.36 kg (3 lb)	**POWER** Battery	**FEATURES** Advanced robotics and artificial intelligence

HOW IT WORKS

Cozmo uses the processing power of its owner's smartphone or tablet to come to life. The owner downloads a free app that connects to Cozmo, and allows them to access multiple features, such as fun games and unique interactions with the robot. The camera on Cozmo's face is sophisticated enough to be able to pick up cues in the robot's environment, such as its cubes, and also to be able to read people's facial expressions.

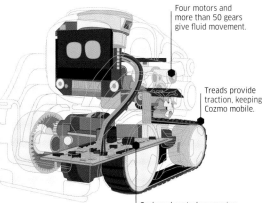

Four motors and more than 50 gears give fluid movement.

Treads provide traction, keeping Cozmo mobile.

On-board central processing unit (CPU) takes care of the data Cozmo picks up.

> **"A robot character with a level of depth and personality that up until now has only been seen in the movies."**
>
> *Boris Sofman*, CEO, **Anki**

Cozmo consists of more than 300 parts, drop-tested to ensure their longevity.

Cozmo's treads work best on clean, flat surfaces.

CODE CONTROL

Cozmo Code Lab is a simplified programming system, allowing even absolute beginners to start coding Cozmo with new content. By dragging and dropping blocks of code on screen, users can explore the robotic functions of animation, facial and object recognition, manipulation, and motion – before Cozmo brings the code to life.

A radio antenna receives signals from the controller on the ground. By altering the speed of the rotors, the operator can change the drone's altitude and direction.

A video camera fixed to the drone gathers aerial images and video.

Controlled machines

On the very bottom of the intelligence scale are controlled machines, which may be very useful but do not think for themselves. They rely, instead, on most of their decisions and their overall control being managed by a human – to the point where many robotics experts do not consider these machines to be robots at all. Drones and unmanned aerial vehicles (UAVs) are under the command of a human operator who communicates with the aircraft via radio signals.

A remote-control twin-axis joystick is used to fly a drone. Using this device, a person can control the speed, altitude, and direction in which the drone flies.

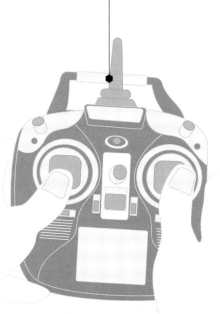

Reactive AI

A reactive artificial intelligence (AI) is a basic form of intelligence, and involves a machine processing data and making decisions within a limited or narrow area of activity. The AI usually does not gain a greater understanding of what it is doing, or form memories of its decisions and actions. Intelligent chess programs often use reactive AI, simulating the outcomes of their next move by calculating how their opponent is most likely to respond. Despite their limitations, they can be highly effective; in 2006 the Deep Fritz reactive AI program defeated the Russian world champion Vladimir Kramnik.

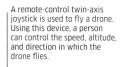

AI analysis

The AI constantly analyses its playing position during a game of draughts. It discounts the move shown above which it predicts would see the opponent take one of its two pieces left.

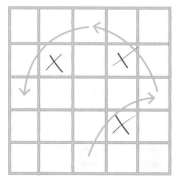

AI decision

In this case, the AI decides on a move that takes three opponent's pieces in one go. Because this will tip the game in its favour, it selects this option. For every move, the AI simulates what moves it can make, and what the opponent is likely to do in response.

Autonomous robots

Autonomous robots are those that can work for long periods of time with no human input or supervision. To be capable of autonomy, a robot needs to be aware of its surroundings, known as perception, which it may achieve through a range of sensors and software. It must be capable of making decisions based on what its sensors perceive, and then be able to carry out actions based on its decisions. Some underwater exploration and many household cleaning robots have high levels of autonomy.

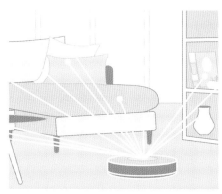

Roomba 980

This vacuum-cleaning robot uses data from its camera and other sensors to build up a detailed, continually updated, visual map of the robot's environment that includes the robot's own position. It is able to choose where to head, pick different cleaning strategies, and avoid obstacles using the map. Its cliff sensors continually scan for drops so it doesn't fall down stairs.

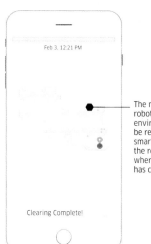

Feb 3, 12:21 PM

The map the robot builds of its environment can be relayed to a smartphone to show the robot's owner where the robot has cleaned.

Clearing Complete!

Mapping

The robot keeps track of where it has already cleaned and of any problems it faced during a cleaning session. The robot can sense when its power is low and autonomously navigates its way to its charging station. After recharging, it resumes cleaning from its previous location.

ROBOT INTELLIGENCE

When we talk about robots being "intelligent", what do we actually mean? Robotics experts have a range of opinions. A simple definition of intelligence is the ability to acquire knowledge and skills, and to be able to apply them in some way, such as to solve a problem or perform useful work. Large numbers of devices we think of as robots are able to gather information using sensors, but not all are able to make decisions and act upon them. Truly intelligent robots can make decisions, adapt to new tasks, and even take information and skills already learned and alter them to tackle new tasks.

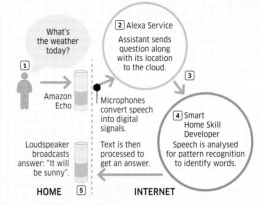

Home assistants

Personal assistant devices appear highly intelligent by recognizing speech and responding to requests and questions from users. In reality, they mostly ferry questions and requests to a powerful artificial intelligence assistant in the cloud – software and services stored on computer networks. There, AI algorithms have built up an understanding of common responses by analysing thousands of previous requests. Solutions are searched for, retrieved, and then relayed back to the personal assistant via the internet.

Automated shops

Artificial intelligence, a wide array of sensors, and special computer algorithms are being brought together to create new hybrid types of intelligence. Thanks to this hybrid intelligence, supermarkets of the future may be without cashiers, shopping baskets, or long queues at checkouts. Instead, you pack your purchases into your own bag as you shop before walking straight out of the store.

3 If a shopper picks up an item and puts it in their bag, sensors alert the store's central inventory computer and the item is added to a list displayed on their smartphone.

4 Behind the scenes, shop staff monitor the data the AI is picking up and the decisions it is making based on this.

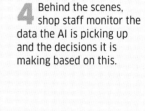

5 Cameras along with weight and pressure sensors in shelves recognize if an item is put back on the shelf, and the product is removed from the shopper's account.

2 Dozens of cameras on ceilings, walls, and shelves identify each shopper using facial recognition and other sensors.

1 Person enters the store by using a smartphone app to open the gate.

6 The person exits the store and the products they leave with are automatically charged to their accounts.

MANUFACTURER	ORIGIN	DEVELOPED	POWER	FEATURES
Leka	France	2015	Battery	Multiple sensors and built-in screen

SOCIAL ROBOT
LEKA

For children with learning difficulties, a smart, cute robot makes a world of difference. Meet Leka, a friendly faced pal for play, learning, and communication. This multi-sensory robotic ball can be programmed to suit individual needs, and produces reports for parents and carers, to benefit long-term learning and development.

BALL OF EMOTION

Leka's face changes expression and the LED lights change colour to convey a range of "emotions" for children to understand. These facial expressions help children recognize and respond to similar displays in other children or adults.

READY FOR ACTION

As soon as the device is picked up, Leka moves from sleepy mode to play time by opening its eyes and smiling. Consistent information is taught alongside regular playtime, as repetition is key for interaction with children who have special needs.

The child's primary senses are engaged with colourful and calming LED lights, soothing sounds, and relaxing vibrations. These are all proven to reduce stress and anxiety levels.

Leka's robotic face can become a screen for photos, videos, or games played using the tablet. The repetitive play of memory games improves the child's learning.

Leka looks sad if thrown or handled badly.

Motors inside Leka enable it to roll around.

> **"Our mission is to help exceptional children live exceptional lives by reducing the learning inequalities..."**
>
> *Ladislas de Toldi,* Founder, **LEKA**

HOW IT WORKS

The child can use a tablet application to make Leka play and move. The child's interactions with both Leka and the tablet app are recorded and turned into data and graphs. Parents and carers can use these to see how well the child is getting on. They can also use a tablet to play games with the child through Leka.

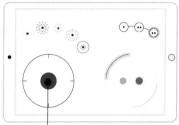

The user can determine the direction of Leka's movement.

Leka smiles to encourage a child's progress.

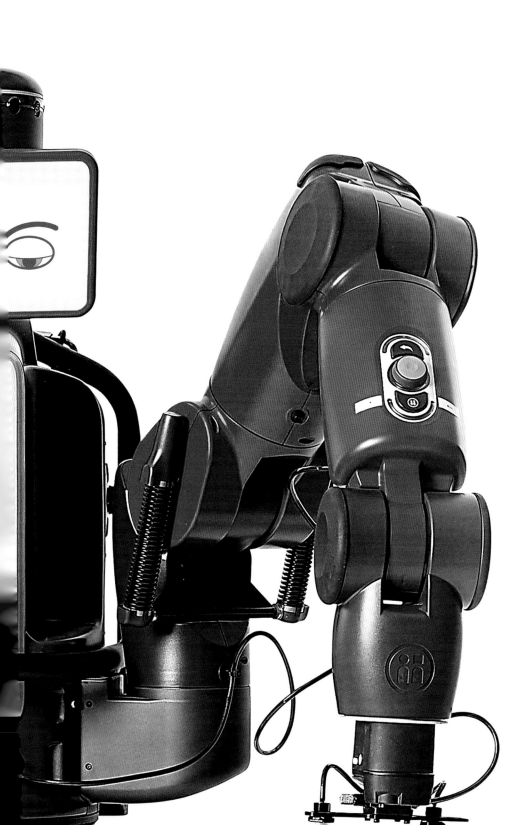

AT WORK

The overwhelming majority of robots are used to do dangerous, dull, or dirty work in factories across the world. Modern robots are highly adept at saving time and effort, and they carry out their tasks without ever getting tired.

MANUFACTURER
KUKA AG

ORIGIN
Germany

RELEASED
2014

WORK ROBOT

LBR iiwa

A new kind of robot is coming to factory floors everywhere. With a soft covering and a slick sensor package, the LBR iiwa (intelligent industrial work assistant) is a lightweight, highly flexible robotic arm that moves fluidly and can be mounted anywhere. A range of safety features makes it a productive co-worker: you can work with it and right next to it, without fear of harm or injury.

> **"**Now that we have such **sensitive robots**, we can develop completely new applications for them.**"**
>
> *Christina Heckl*, Engineer, **KUKA**

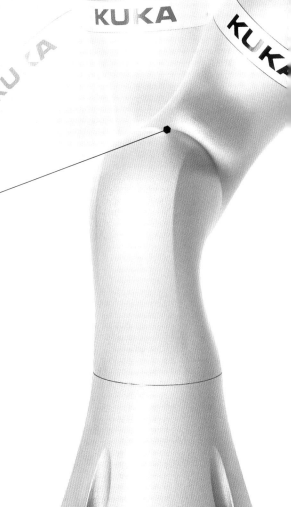

Special sensors in each joint stop the arm from moving if they detect any unexpected contact with an object.

IN CONTROL

LBR iiwa can be programmed in advance, and either taught by demonstration or instructed directly using a SmartPAD controller. This rugged touchscreen device weighs 1.1 kg (2.4 lb) and communicates wirelessly with the robot. Jog keys to the left of the screen allow each of the robotic arm's joints to be guided to within fractions of a centimetre.

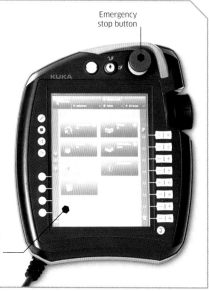

Emergency stop button

The touchscreen displays menu options and icons.

HEIGHT	WEIGHT	POWER	FEATURES
1.3 m (4.3 ft)	30 kg (66 lb)	Mains electricity	Can plot its own path and actions

This elbow is one of seven moving joints that gives the arm great flexibility.

The wrist can be fitted with different tools, including grippers for lifting small, delicate objects, a riveter for joining sheets of metal, and an electric power-wrench for tightening nuts and bolts.

The arm is made from lightweight aluminium.

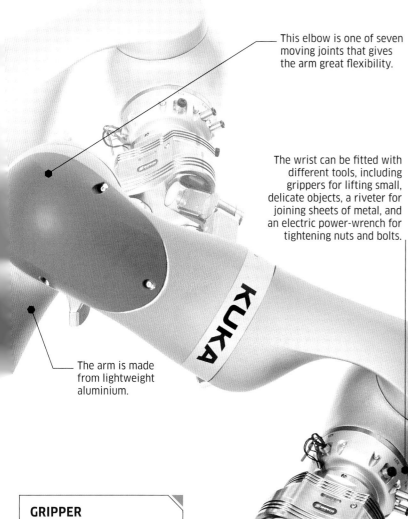

HOW IT WORKS

The robot's seven joints each have a wide range of motion, and are powered by high-precision electric motors. These work together to let the robot reach around corners and work in tight spaces. The arm movements are accurate to within 0.1 mm (0.004 in), which makes it ideal for assembling small, complex objects such as electronics.

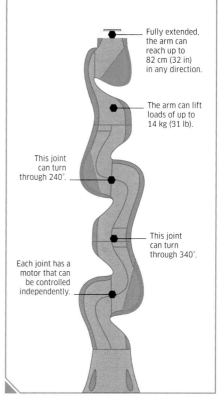

Fully extended, the arm can reach up to 82 cm (32 in) in any direction.

The arm can lift loads of up to 14 kg (31 lb).

This joint can turn through 240°.

This joint can turn through 340°.

Each joint has a motor that can be controlled independently.

GRIPPER

The robot's cushioned grippers can close and grip an object in just 18 milliseconds. The amount of force they use can be adjusted by programming or the SmartPAD controller.

The force of the gripper reduces when handling delicate objects like an egg, but it can be increased when the robot is tightening fastenings or handling heavy, robust objects.

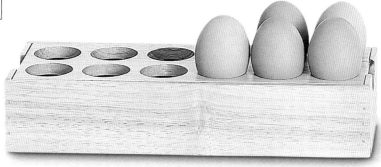

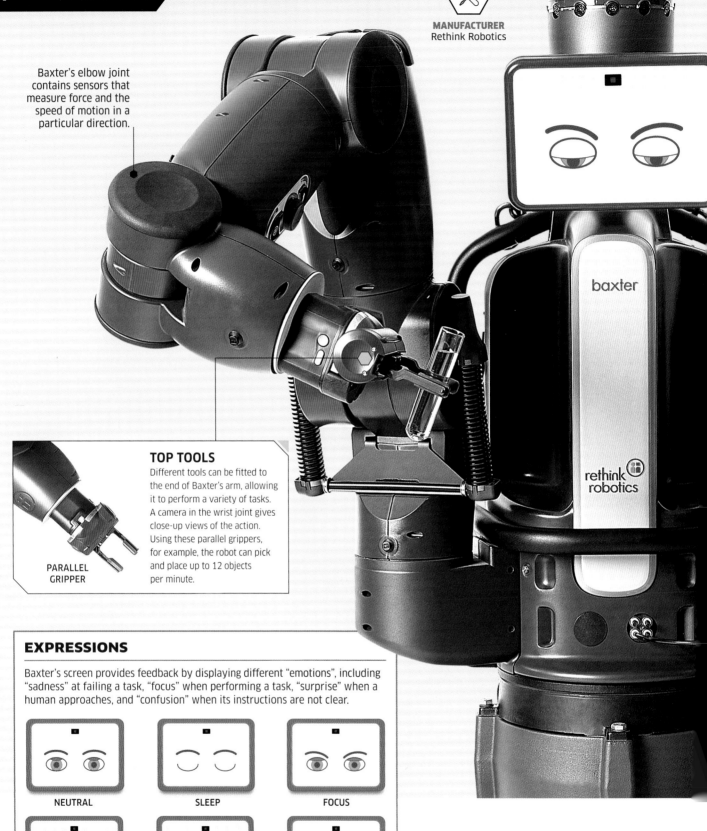

MANUFACTURER
Rethink Robotics

Baxter's elbow joint contains sensors that measure force and the speed of motion in a particular direction.

baxter

rethink robotics

TOP TOOLS

Different tools can be fitted to the end of Baxter's arm, allowing it to perform a variety of tasks. A camera in the wrist joint gives close-up views of the action. Using these parallel grippers, for example, the robot can pick and place up to 12 objects per minute.

PARALLEL GRIPPER

EXPRESSIONS

Baxter's screen provides feedback by displaying different "emotions", including "sadness" at failing a task, "focus" when performing a task, "surprise" when a human approaches, and "confusion" when its instructions are not clear.

NEUTRAL

SLEEP

FOCUS

SURPRISE

CONFUSION

SADNESS

ORIGIN
USA

RELEASED
2012

HEIGHT
1.9 m (6.25 ft)
with pedestal

WEIGHT
138.7 kg (306 lb)
with pedestal

POWER
Battery

FEATURES
Motorized joints equipped
with sensors that detect
resistance and collisions

COLLABORATIVE ROBOT
BAXTER

One of the most versatile collaborative robots,
Baxter is an easy-to-train twin-armed robot
with a very expressive face. Five cameras
mounted in its head, body, and arms, along
with force sensors in its joints, work together
to help Baxter avoid banging into things,
especially humans. And if it does bump into
something, it stops moving instantly, making
it safe for humans to work with it.

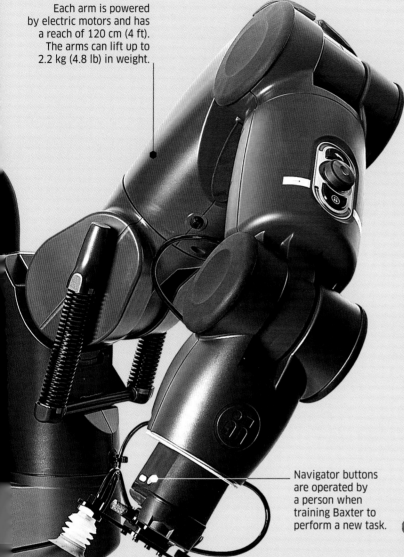

Each arm is powered
by electric motors and has
a reach of 120 cm (4 ft).
The arms can lift up to
2.2 kg (4.8 lb) in weight.

Navigator buttons
are operated by
a person when
training Baxter to
perform a new task.

Vacuum grippers use
a pump to create suction
to grip delicate objects.

HOW IT WORKS

Baxter can be taught a task easily without the
need for any computer programming. Switched into
training mode, the robot is physically guided by
a human trainer through a set of actions, which
it remembers and can repeat accurately.

When teaching Baxter to
pick and place objects from
a conveyor belt into a box,
the trainer swings its arm
over the object and clicks
the navigator button.

Baxter's wrist camera
focuses on an object and
displays it on screen. Once
the trainer confirms it
is the right object, Baxter
grips and picks it up.

A pedestal with
wheels allows Baxter
to move easily.

FRONT VIEW

The trainer swings the
arm over to the object's
final destination. Baxter
uses its sensors to guide
the object into the box.
Once the task is saved,
Baxter can repeat it
over and over.

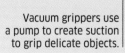

Programming by pendant

In this method of programming, a human operator controls the robot using a handheld device called a teaching pendant. Controls on the pendant allow the operator to instruct the robot where to move from point to point, and what actions to perform, in a sequence. These instructions are stored as a program, which enables the robot to repeat the actions and so perform the real task when the program is run back. Large programs are often split up into smaller units called sub-programs. This makes it easier for the operator to teach the robot and simpler to make changes later. The teaching pendant method is commonly used for industrial robots that perform spot-welding of vehicles, spray-painting, picking and placing objects, and loading and unloading other factory machines.

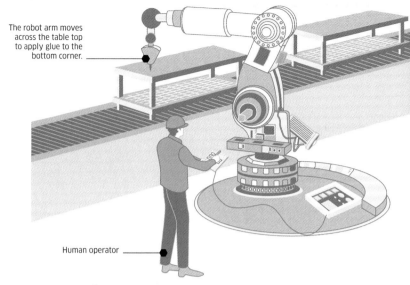

The robot arm moves across the table top to apply glue to the bottom corner.

Human operator

1 Teaching

Holding a teaching pendant, the operator commands this industrial robot to apply glue to each corner of a table on a production line. The robot is instructed to move relatively slowly during the teaching process between points to ensure safety and accuracy.

Pendant features

Teaching pendants can be wired with a cable attached to a robot or its computer workstation, or wireless, communicating with the robot via radio signals. Modern pendants take advantage of advances in computer technology. They offer easier input methods and ways of controlling ever-more complex robots, and the tasks they are being taught to perform. Pendants tend to be rugged, dustproof, and resistant to knocks and splashes of liquid. Pendants are tailored to the tasks the robots they control. They have a number of features that can be found in isolation or combined to aid operators.

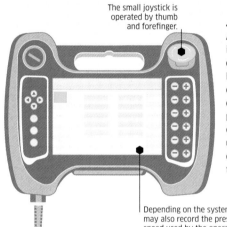

The small joystick is operated by thumb and forefinger.

Joystick

A joystick is a simple controller or input device. The most basic allow the operator to move something up, down, left, or right, and the most advanced offer precise 360° movement. Pendant operators may guide the robot from point to point using the joystick. At each arrival point, the operator can use jog keys on this and other types of pendant to make small adjustments to the robot's positioning.

Depending on the system, the program may also record the pressure and speed used by the operator when inputting instructions.

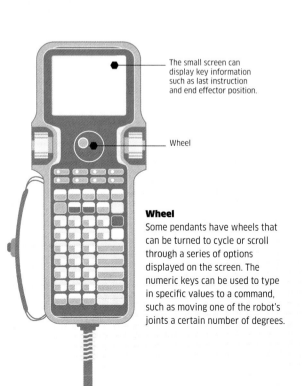

The small screen can display key information such as last instruction and end effector position.

Wheel

Wheel

Some pendants have wheels that can be turned to cycle or scroll through a series of options displayed on the screen. The numeric keys can be used to type in specific values to a command, such as moving one of the robot's joints a certain number of degrees.

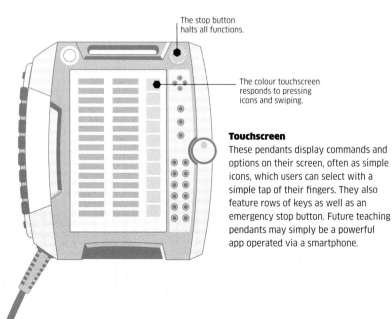

The stop button halts all functions.

The colour touchscreen responds to pressing icons and swiping.

Touchscreen

These pendants display commands and options on their screen, often as simple icons, which users can select with a simple tap of their fingers. They also feature rows of keys as well as an emergency stop button. Future teaching pendants may simply be a powerful app operated via a smartphone.

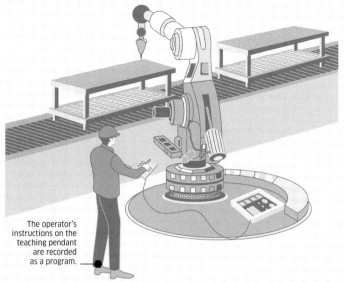

The operator's instructions on the teaching pendant are recorded as a program.

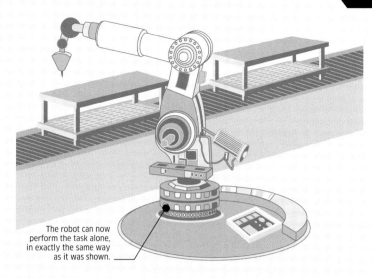

The robot can now perform the task alone, in exactly the same way as it was shown.

2 Recording and testing
At each teaching stage, the robot records its movements and actions, and stores them as a program. After recording, the robot may be instructed to run through the program again to test it. The operator can stop the program at any stage to edit and modify it to obtain the necessary precision and ideal speed of operation.

3 Action
With modifications and testing complete, the teaching pendant can be disconnected and the robot can get to work. The speed of movement of the robot's parts may have been increased to perform the task more rapidly, but also to match the speeds of other robots and machines working on the production line.

ONLINE PROGRAMMING

A brand new robot rolls off a production line. It may be bright and shiny, but it isn't much use until it receives its instructions. Online programming is where the robot is programmed directly at its workplace, such as on a factory's production line. The programming may be used to instruct a brand new robot, or change the way a robot already in place functions. Online programming can be time-consuming. Fortunately, ways have been found of simplifying and speeding up the process.

Programming by demonstration

As robot technology advances, one increasingly popular method of online programming has become lead-through programming. This involves a human operator demonstrating or even describing a task to a robot, usually by physically moving it through all the actions required, in the correct order. The robot stores each instruction and movement in its memory and can repeat them accurately to perform the task. This form of instructing the robot requires little or no programming knowledge in the operator, but the operator must be skilled at performing the task the robot is to copy.

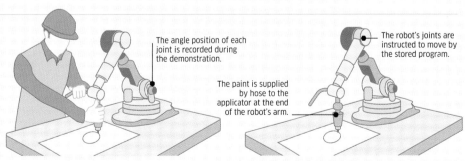

The angle position of each joint is recorded during the demonstration.

The robot's joints are instructed to move by the stored program.

The paint is supplied by hose to the applicator at the end of the robot's arm.

1 Demonstration
The human operator guides the robot arm through the movements needed to create the lettering and numbering on a sign. At each stage of the task, the robot records and stores in memory the position of its parts and the actions performed.

2 Action
When commanded to do so, the robot can replay the steps involved in the task to repeat it at full speed, and with unerring accuracy, time and time again. This method of programming tends to be quicker than using teaching pendants.

MANUFACTURER
Intuitive Surgical, Inc.

ORIGIN
USA

RELEASED
2000

POWER
Mains electricity

PILOTED ROBOT

DA VINCI SURGICAL SYSTEM

Many people might find a robot surgeon to be a scary thought, but the Da Vinci Surgical System is no ordinary robot. The system can move tiny surgical instruments precisely, sometimes moving a tool as small as a grain of rice to within fractions of a millimetre. It cannot conduct operations autonomously, though – it is instead a tool used by a human surgeon. Nearly 4,000 Da Vinci Surgical System robots are in use across the globe, racking up more than three million operations worldwide since 2000.

The motor-powered joints are each capable of a wide range of movement.

HOW IT WORKS

Sitting at the console, a surgeon instructs the robot using foot pedals and hand controls. The surgeon's movements are mirrored by the robot's arms instantly as they manipulate tiny instruments inside the patient. At all times, staff are on hand to monitor the patient, while views of the operation inside the body are displayed on a screen.

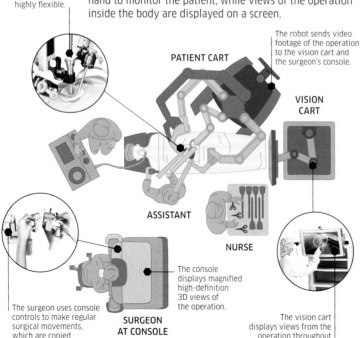

The tiny wrist instruments are highly flexible.

PATIENT CART

The robot sends video footage of the operation to the vision cart and the surgeon's console.

VISION CART

ASSISTANT

NURSE

SURGEON AT CONSOLE

The console displays magnified high-definition 3D views of the operation.

The surgeon uses console controls to make regular surgical movements, which are copied accurately by the robot.

The vision cart displays views from the operation throughout the operating room.

Each arm's scale of movement can be adjusted by the surgeon so that it moves only a fraction of the distance the surgeon's hand moves, allowing a finer control of the robot during an operation.

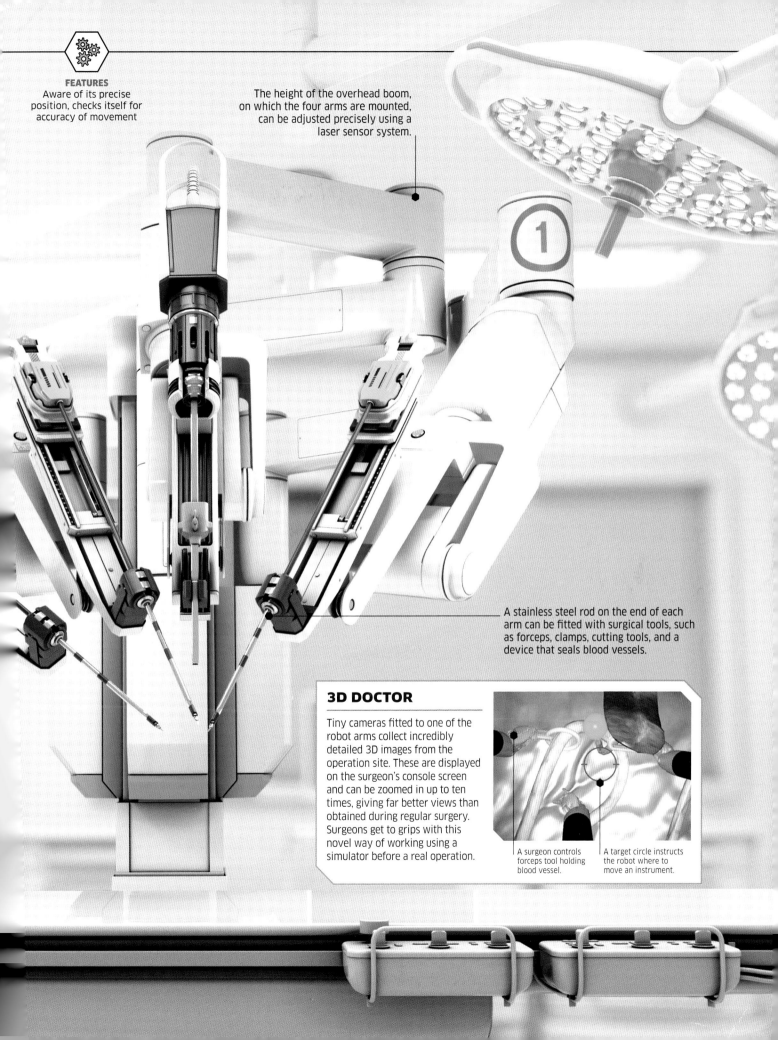

Aware of its precise position, checks itself for accuracy of movement

The height of the overhead boom, on which the four arms are mounted, can be adjusted precisely using a laser sensor system.

A stainless steel rod on the end of each arm can be fitted with surgical tools, such as forceps, clamps, cutting tools, and a device that seals blood vessels.

3D DOCTOR

Tiny cameras fitted to one of the robot arms collect incredibly detailed 3D images from the operation site. These are displayed on the surgeon's console screen and can be zoomed in up to ten times, giving far better views than obtained during regular surgery. Surgeons get to grips with this novel way of working using a simulator before a real operation.

A surgeon controls forceps tool holding blood vessel.

A target circle instructs the robot where to move an instrument.

VALUED VALET

Electronic valet **Stan** can use sensor technology to lift and carry your car to the nearest parking space. This valet service is second to none – customers simply drop their car at the airport, confirm the reservation on a touchscreen, lock their car, and leave the rest to the robot. Stan is currently in operation at Charles de Gaulle airport in Paris, France, with each robot overseeing up to 400 parking spaces.

▶ Stan slides underneath the four wheels of the car and brings it to the car park.

GREAT GUARD

Just like a security guard, **Cobalt's** role is to protect offices, businesses, and warehouses. This indoor robot patrols buildings day and night to report on suspicious activity. Cobalt has 60 sensors, cameras, and audio equipment that can detect a multitude of problems, including open doors, leaking pipes, or unexpected visitors. It also features detectors for carbon monoxide and smoke, as well as a scanner to read and verify workers' identification badges.

◀ This human-sized robot has a touchscreen display for live interaction with people.

▲ Cobalt can patrol at a walking pace without interrupting daily human activities.

FLEXIBLE ARM

Integrating robots and lasers has resulted in **LaserSnake**, a groundbreaking technology for use in dangerous places. The snake-like robotic arm contains flexible joints, HD cameras, and LED lights, while the electronics and control systems are operated remotely. When decommissioning nuclear cells at power plants, LaserSnake can cut through and dismantle radioactive components without any risk to human life, putting safety first while also keeping costs down.

High-power laser cutting head

▶ LaserSnake has a hollow centre so a variety of cables, hoses, and lasers can be attached to it.

HARD AT WORK

With modern life being so hectic, new ways to save time, effort, and money are always welcome. Robots are increasingly being used to share the load. Studies have predicted that by 2030, hundreds of millions of robots will work alongside human employees. From basic tasks such as stacking supermarket shelves to dangerous assignments in nuclear power plants, the latest robots can get the job done.

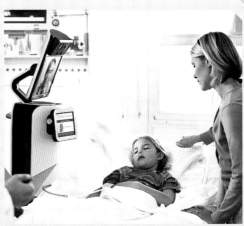

▲ A two-way camera system enables remote interaction between a doctor and a patient.

SUPERMARKET HELPER

Shelf-stacking supremo **Tally** can work 12-hour shifts alongside colleagues and customers. Using cameras and sensors, this grocery bot inspects the aisles for products past their date, in the wrong place, or running low in stock. Tests have shown that Tally can count and check 20,000 items with an impressive accuracy rate of more than 96 per cent.

HOSPITAL HELPER

RP-VITA is a robot designed to help medical professionals share healthcare information with colleagues and patients. It is called a "remote" robot, as it allows doctors to look after patients and access their information despite not being physically with them. It can get this information in a variety of ways, including connecting remotely to medical machines, such as digital stethoscopes and ultrasounds. RP-VITA is already in use in some US hospitals where doctors can monitor their patients from anywhere in the world.

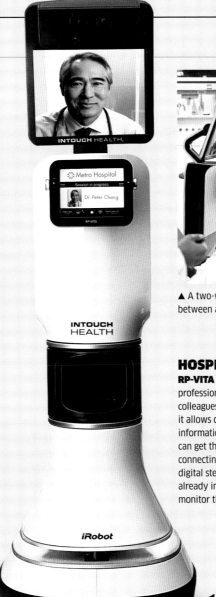

▲ Tally moves through the shopping aisles on a wheeled base.

◄ An automatic docking function keeps RP-VITA charged permanently during medical emergencies.

SURVEILLANCE SPHERE

This sphere-shaped, **GroundBot** comes equipped with cameras and sensors, bringing increased security to public places, including airports, harbours, and warehouses – all at a fraction of the normal cost. Whether remote-controlled or programmed to use GPS navigation systems, the lightweight design of the robot enables silent surveillance at speeds of 10 km/h (6 mph) for up to 16 hours.

▲ All data collected by Tally is accessed by shop owners on a cloud-based application.

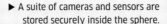

▶ A suite of cameras and sensors are stored securely inside the sphere.

OFFLINE PROGRAMMING

Robots need to be given detailed instructions before they can perform a task. Offline programming is where programmers use software to design, code, and debug (fix) a program in advance of installing it onto the robot. Online programming – where a robot is taught by an operator to do a task – can be time-consuming. Offline programming can save time as the programs can be worked on independently of the robot, so that the instructions are uploaded to the robot only when they are ready. Programs may be uploaded to the robot wirelessly, or directly through a physical link such as a memory card or cable.

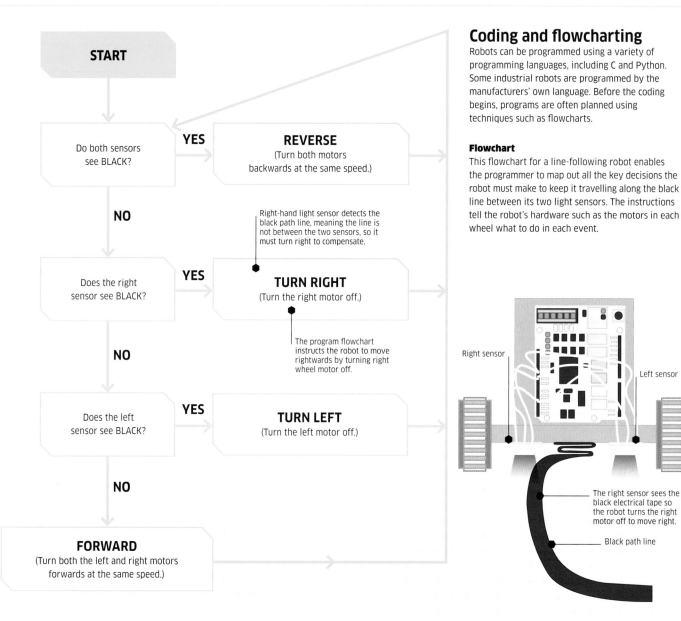

START

Do both sensors see BLACK? — YES → **REVERSE** (Turn both motors backwards at the same speed.)

NO

Does the right sensor see BLACK? — YES → **TURN RIGHT** (Turn the right motor off.)

Right-hand light sensor detects the black path line, meaning the line is not between the two sensors, so it must turn right to compensate.

The program flowchart instructs the robot to move rightwards by turning right wheel motor off.

NO

Does the left sensor see BLACK? — YES → **TURN LEFT** (Turn the left motor off.)

NO

FORWARD (Turn both the left and right motors forwards at the same speed.)

Coding and flowcharting

Robots can be programmed using a variety of programming languages, including C and Python. Some industrial robots are programmed by the manufacturers' own language. Before the coding begins, programs are often planned using techniques such as flowcharts.

Flowchart

This flowchart for a line-following robot enables the programmer to map out all the key decisions the robot must make to keep it travelling along the black line between its two light sensors. The instructions tell the robot's hardware such as the motors in each wheel what to do in each event.

Right sensor

Left sensor

The right sensor sees the black electrical tape so the robot turns the right motor off to move right.

Black path line

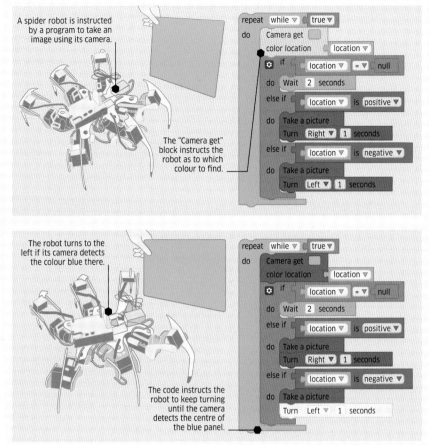

A spider robot is instructed by a program to take an image using its camera.

The "Camera get" block instructs the robot as to which colour to find.

The robot turns to the left if its camera detects the colour blue there.

The code instructs the robot to keep turning until the camera detects the centre of the blue panel.

Block by block

As robot numbers boom, easier, more universal ways of programming are being developed to enable more people to program them. One such example is the Robot Operating System (ROS) – a collection of tools that coders can use to construct their own programs. Robot Blockly is based on ROS but makes coding easier and more user-friendly by portraying commands as colourful blocks, in a similar way to the Scratch programming language. The blocks can be clipped together to produce sequences of commands and decisions, such as the following code to make a robot move each time it spots the colour blue.

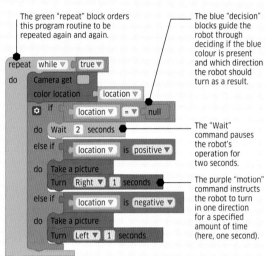

The green "repeat" block orders this program routine to be repeated again and again.

The blue "decision" blocks guide the robot through deciding if the blue colour is present and which direction the robot should turn as a result.

The "Wait" command pauses the robot's operation for two seconds.

The purple "motion" command instructs the robot to turn in one direction for a specified amount of time (here, one second).

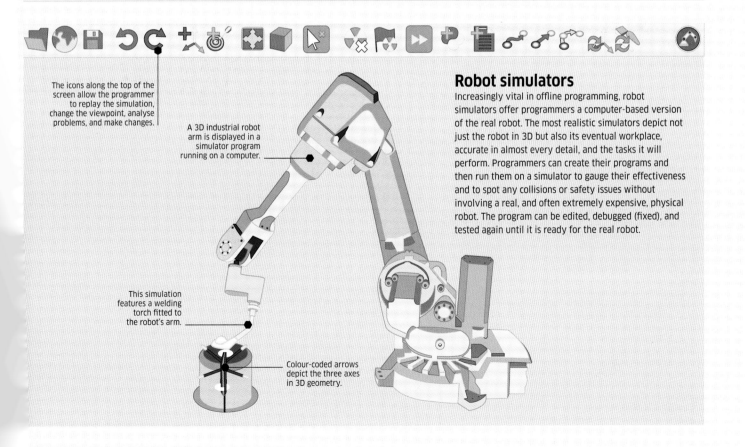

The icons along the top of the screen allow the programmer to replay the simulation, change the viewpoint, analyse problems, and make changes.

A 3D industrial robot arm is displayed in a simulator program running on a computer.

This simulation features a welding torch fitted to the robot's arm.

Colour-coded arrows depict the three axes in 3D geometry.

Robot simulators

Increasingly vital in offline programming, robot simulators offer programmers a computer-based version of the real robot. The most realistic simulators depict not just the robot in 3D but also its eventual workplace, accurate in almost every detail, and the tasks it will perform. Programmers can create their programs and then run them on a simulator to gauge their effectiveness and to spot any collisions or safety issues without involving a real, and often extremely expensive, physical robot. The program can be edited, debugged (fixed), and tested again until it is ready for the real robot.

MANUFACTURER	ORIGIN	RELEASED	HEIGHT	FEATURES
K-Team and Harvard University	Switzerland and USA	2011	34 mm (1.33 in)	Can work together in large numbers autonomously

The charging hook forms a circuit with the robot's legs, allowing the battery to be recharged.

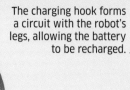

These pins can be connected to a cable to download new instructions or programs.

SWARM ROBOT
KILOBOTS

Large groups of mobile robots could perform dozens of useful jobs in the future – from cleaning up disaster sites to exploring distant worlds in space, but researchers struggle to obtain enough costly bots to experiment with. Kilobots are small, simple, and cheap, and can be programmed individually or in large numbers simultaneously, using infrared signals from an overhead wireless controller. They communicate using infrared signals to gauge their distances from one another and can be programmed to form shapes, or follow a path or a lead robot. It's quite a sight when hundreds of these robots all swarm and work together.

CONTROL BOARD

The board at the bottom houses the robot's microprocessor controller and its infrared communications system. Each Kilobot's infrared transmitter can send a signal, which is bounced off the floor to reach another Kilobot's infrared receiver, up to 7 cm (2.75 in) away.

Infrared receiver

Infrared transmitter

TINY BOT

Two vibration motors (originally from mobile phones) power Kilobot's movement. When they both vibrate, the robot moves forwards on its stiff legs at speeds of up to 1 cm (0.4 in) per second. This low-power solution means that a small 3.7 volt battery can power the robot for up to 2.5 hours of action before it needs a recharge.

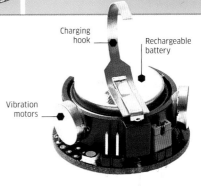

Charging hook

Rechargeable battery

Vibration motors

Rigid legs

COLLECTIVE ACTION

A gaggle of Kilobots may be spread randomly, but on command, they quickly band together, tottering along on their vibrating legs. Computer algorithms in these low-cost robots plot paths and stop any rogue robots from veering off course. It doesn't take long for these ingenious little machines to complete a joint task, such as 85 Kilobots forming an arrow shape.

EVERYDAY BOTS

Robots are gradually becoming part of our everyday lives. From providing us with information to helping us learn and have fun, bots are starting to become essential to humans. In the future, it may be normal to have a meal cooked by a robot, or even to have a conversation with one.

MANUFACTURER
SoftBank Robotics

ORIGIN
France

LISTENING IN

Pepper has four directional microphones in its head. These help the bot detect where sound is coming from. They also help Pepper identify emotions in someone's voice and make conversation in response.

Sounds and music play through the in-ear speakers.

Pepper is equipped with two HD cameras (in the mouth and forehead) and one 3D sensor (behind the eyes) that help it identify movement, spot objects, and recognize emotions on someone's face.

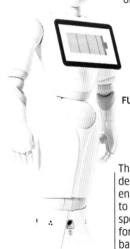

FULL VIEW

Three specially designed wheels enable Pepper to rotate on the spot and move forwards and backwards.

TABLET

The touchscreen tablet mounted on Pepper's chest can be used to display whatever information Pepper's controller desires, such as images, videos, webpages, or maps. It can also be used to collect information from the humans Pepper communicates with.

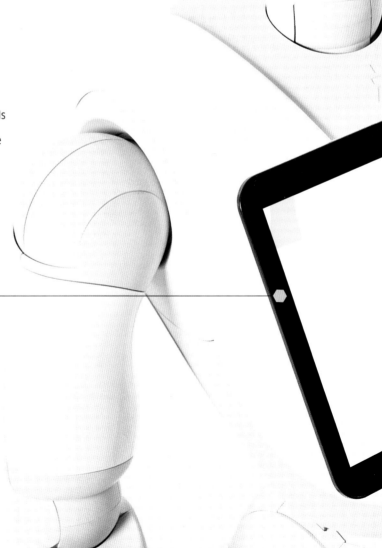

RELEASED	HEIGHT	WEIGHT	POWER	FEATURES
2015	1.2 m (4 ft)	28 kg (62 lb)	Battery	Can recognize and respond to people's emotions in real time

SOCIAL ROBOT
PEPPER

This communicative robot was designed to interact with and help humans. According to its makers, Pepper is the first humanoid robot capable of reading people's emotions and responding to them in real time. It is packed with two ultrasound transmitters and receivers, six laser sensors, and three obstacle detectors. Since its commercial release in 2015, Pepper has been hard at work at all manner of jobs in restaurants, banks, hotels, hospitals, and shopping malls.

GREAT GRIP
Pepper's hands are made to be soft and flexible. Its fingers can bend easily and are covered in rubber to improve the bot's grip. The rubber makes it safe for a child to hold hands with Pepper.

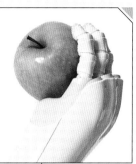

The touch sensors in the arms and on the hands are used when playing games and for social interaction.

❝Pepper… is a genuine humanoid companion, created to communicate with you in the most natural and intuitive way.❞
SoftBank Robotics

REACTIONS

Pepper is designed to look and move like a human, so that people interact with it as if it were alive. Its range of arm movements is natural and smooth, thanks to a system of joints in the shoulders and elbows. These enable the bot to raise its arms, roll its shoulders, and twist its wrists. Pepper also has joints in its neck and waist.

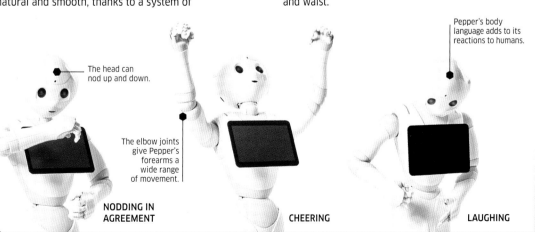

The head can nod up and down.

The elbow joints give Pepper's forearms a wide range of movement.

Pepper's body language adds to its reactions to humans.

NODDING IN AGREEMENT

CHEERING

LAUGHING

HOME-HELP ROBOT

GITA

Forget backpacks, carriers, and suitcases –
Gita is definitely your bag. This round, rolling
robot takes a load off while following in your
footsteps, and uses gyroscopes to keep your stuff
upright. Heavy goods and personal items can be
stored inside, leaving you happily hands-free.
Once packed and ready to go, the high-tech moving
storage box uses you as a guide to map out its
surroundings and remember the route for future
trips. Best of all, there are no tired feet, because
Gita can keep going all day!

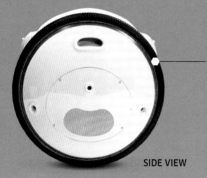

Two large tyres
help Gita move
freely and easily.

SIDE VIEW

HOW GYROSCOPES WORK

Robots, ships, and aircraft use gyroscopes for
stability. These mechanical navigational devices
balance moving objects when they change course.
A spinning disc, called a rotor, mounted inside
a gyroscope frame can move in any direction.
However, an attached ring called a gimbal keeps
the axis pointing in the same direction, regardless
of internal movement. Gita uses gyroscopes to
keep its contents upright, so they do not move
too much when in transit.

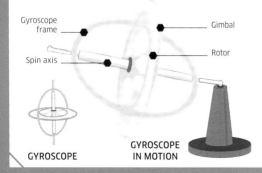

Gyroscope
frame

Gimbal

Rotor

Spin axis

GYROSCOPE

GYROSCOPE
IN MOTION

Each wheel is fitted with
LED lights that change
colour: blue when idle,
white when in transit,
yellow when the battery is
running low, and red when
something has gone wrong.

MANUFACTURER	**ORIGIN**	**HEIGHT**	**POWER**	**FEATURES**
Piaggio Fast Forward	USA	66 cm (26 in)	Eight hours battery life at normal walking speed	Cameras, sensors, and navigation system

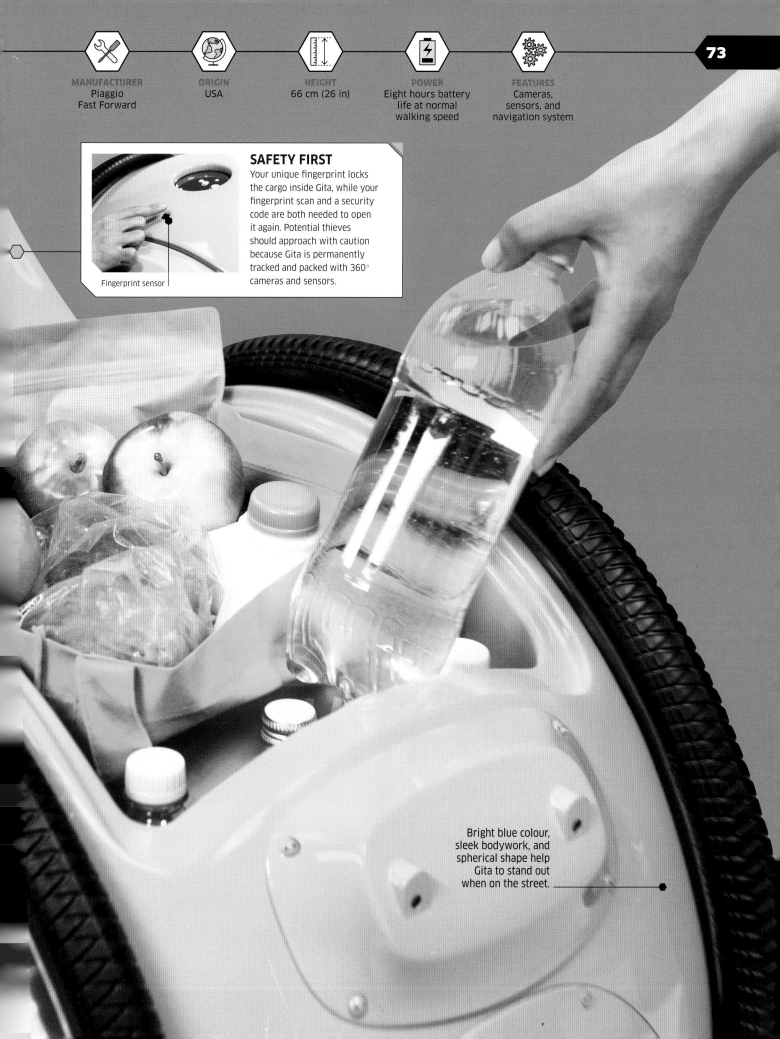

SAFETY FIRST
Your unique fingerprint locks the cargo inside Gita, while your fingerprint scan and a security code are both needed to open it again. Potential thieves should approach with caution because Gita is permanently tracked and packed with 360° cameras and sensors.

Fingerprint sensor

Bright blue colour, sleek bodywork, and spherical shape help Gita to stand out when on the street.

HIGHER INTELLIGENCE

From driverless cars that predict traffic movement to robotic assistants equipped with intelligent speech recognition, robots are being designed to learn from their experiences, just like humans. Some can apply the knowledge they gain to improve the way they perform their tasks, or even to new situations they haven't encountered before. The goal is to develop robots that can learn, adapt to, and use new information the way humans can. Although progress has been made, even the most intelligent robots can't match the all-round versatility of humans.

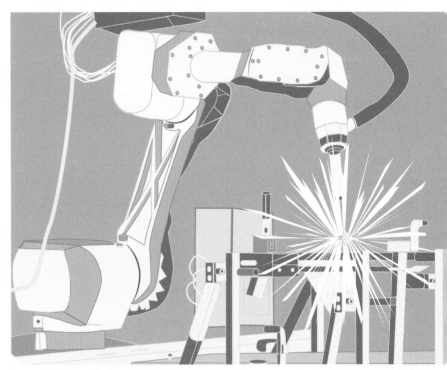

Welding
An artificially-intelligent robot arm of the future welds metal parts together. Able to draw on its memories, it improves and refin how it welds autonomously.

General artificial intelligence

The ultimate goal for many working with intelligent robots is to build machines that match (or even exceed) the sort of creative, flexible, and wide-ranging intelligence that humans have. For a machine to display a general artificial intelligence, it would need to be capable of planning, reasoning, and solving problems autonomously, just like humans do. It would also need to be able to recall useful information from past experiences and apply it to wildly different new situations. Such robots would be incredibly useful, capable of tackling new tasks without being reprogrammed and able to interact with people and other machines with ease.

Painting
The same robot might then, without reprogramming, be able to work as an artist. As soon as it sensed and recognized the paintbrush in its gripper, it began solving problems and making decisions in order to paint an attractive artwork.

Machine learning

Machine learning is the ability for a robot or computer to learn from data rather than be directly programmed by humans. It means that the machine senses patterns or gains important knowledge from the information it gathers from its sensors. Machine learning has enabled robots' vision systems to learn how to sort, group, and identify objects. In the example below, a robot uses data to construct and compare depth maps to recognize a particular household object.

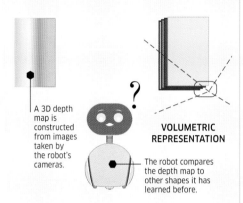

A 3D depth map is constructed from images taken by the robot's cameras.

VOLUMETRIC REPRESENTATION

The robot compares the depth map to other shapes it has learned before.

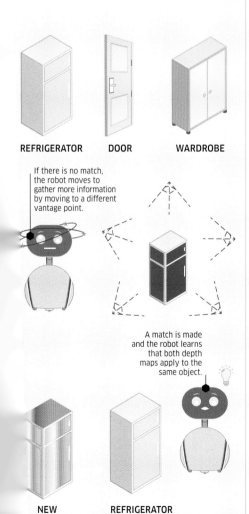

REFRIGERATOR   DOOR   WARDROBE

If there is no match, the robot moves to gather more information by moving to a different vantage point.

A match is made and the robot learns that both depth maps apply to the same object.

NEW DEPTH MAP   REFRIGERATOR

Deep learning

Learning how to learn is a key step on the path to artificial general intelligence. Deep learning involves attempting to give robots the sorts of skills required for them to learn and master a new task for themselves, with little or no human intervention. In some cases, it can mean the robot is equipped to learn by trial and error, testing out lots of different approaches and remembering and learning from all its previous attempts. In this example, a robot is attempting to learn how to pick up objects.

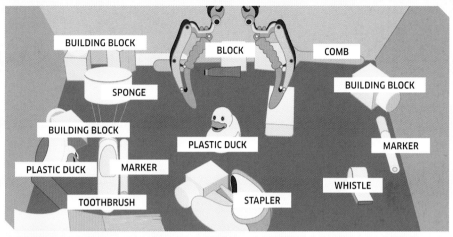

BUILDING BLOCK   BLOCK   COMB
SPONGE   BUILDING BLOCK
BUILDING BLOCK   PLASTIC DUCK   MARKER
PLASTIC DUCK   MARKER   WHISTLE
TOOTHBRUSH   STAPLER

Surveying the scene
A deep-learning robot views a scene and uses depth perception to isolate individual objects from one another, before attempting to recognize them.

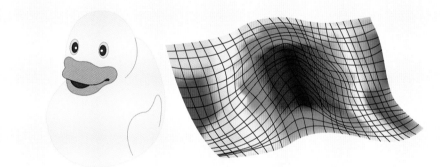

Depth mapping
The robot makes depth maps of the objects and seeks out any suitable raised areas it can grip.

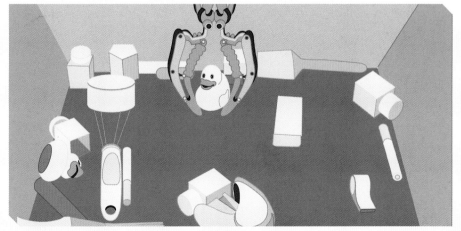

Attempting the task
The robot attempts to grip an object. If it fails, it may adjust its grip force, try again from a different angle, or pick another part to grip. Successes and failures are fed back and stored in the memory so that the robot can learn from trial and error. Eventually, the robot will learn how to interact with each object.

MANUFACTURER
RobotCub Consortium
and Italian Institute
of Technology

ORIGIN
Italy

RELEASED
2004

HEIGHT
104 cm (41 in)

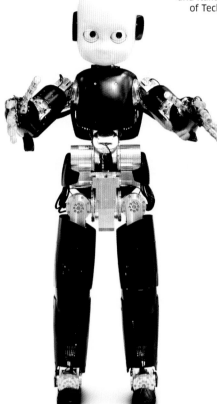
FULL VIEW

HUMANOID ROBOT
iCub

About the size of a 3-year-old and just as curious, iCub uses its body to explore the world. Some 30 of these ground-breaking robo-toddlers are being experimented with in robotics labs around the world. The ultimate goal is to create a truly cognitive bot – one that can learn, understand, and adapt to all sorts of tasks, just like humans do. So far, one iCub can play the drums while another has mastered the complex game of chess. Checkmate!

More than **30 iCub** robots are in **operation** around the **world**.

The jointed thumb can bend in similar ways to a human thumb to help grasp and hold objects.

HOW IT WORKS

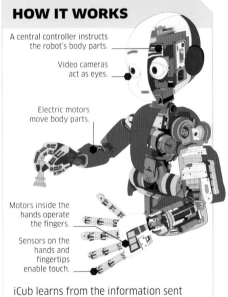

A central controller instructs the robot's body parts.

Video cameras act as eyes.

Electric motors move body parts.

Motors inside the hands operate the fingers.

Sensors on the hands and fingertips enable touch.

iCub learns from the information sent to it by its vision, audio, and tactile sensors to recognize and understand objects and learn the nuances of how best to interact with them. The sensors in each joint give it a sense of proprioception – knowing where all of its body parts are as it moves.

FACIAL EXPRESSIONS

Happy today or feeling grumpy? iCub lets others know its mood using a range of preset facial expressions. These are generated by LED lights buried under its face, which light up to demonstrate iCub's "emotions": it responds to how well it thinks a task is going.

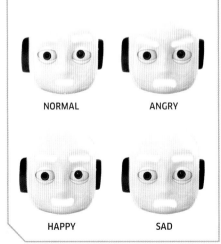

NORMAL

ANGRY

HAPPY

SAD

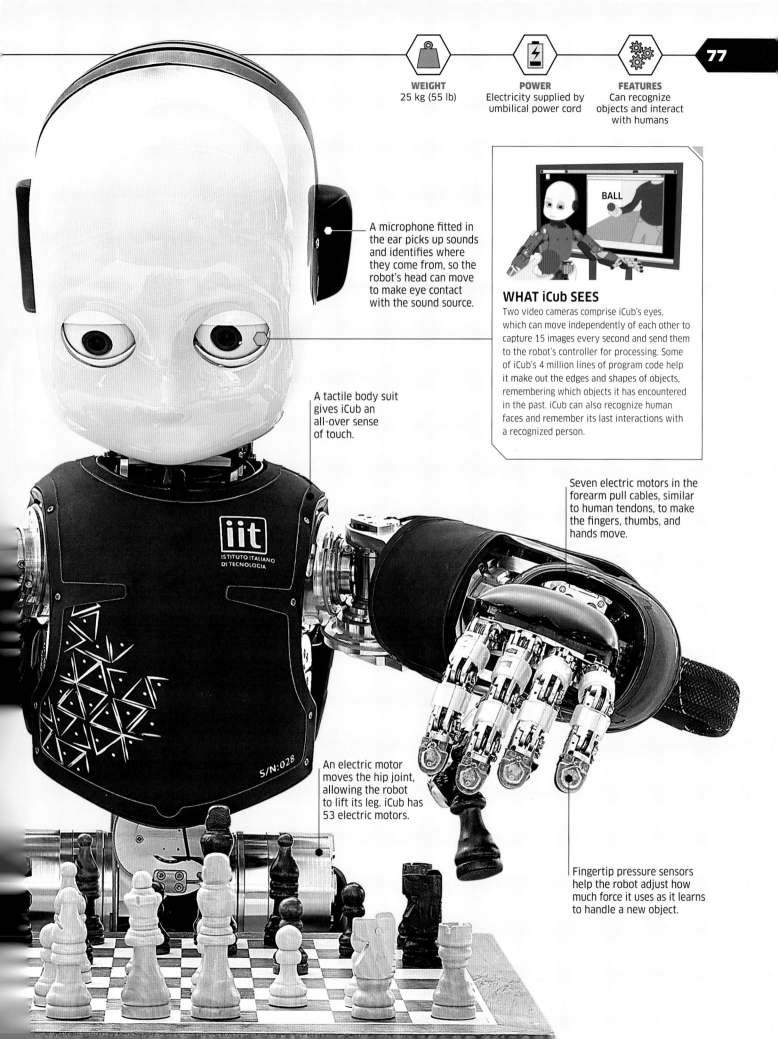

WEIGHT
25 kg (55 lb)

POWER
Electricity supplied by
umbilical power cord

FEATURES
Can recognize
objects and interact
with humans

A microphone fitted in
the ear picks up sounds
and identifies where
they come from, so the
robot's head can move
to make eye contact
with the sound source.

BALL

WHAT iCub SEES

Two video cameras comprise iCub's eyes,
which can move independently of each other to
capture 15 images every second and send them
to the robot's controller for processing. Some
of iCub's 4 million lines of program code help
it make out the edges and shapes of objects,
remembering which objects it has encountered
in the past. iCub can also recognize human
faces and remember its last interactions with
a recognized person.

A tactile body suit
gives iCub an
all-over sense
of touch.

Seven electric motors in the
forearm pull cables, similar
to human tendons, to make
the fingers, thumbs, and
hands move.

iit
ISTITUTO ITALIANO
DI TECNOLOGIA

S/N:028

An electric motor
moves the hip joint,
allowing the robot
to lift its leg. iCub has
53 electric motors.

Fingertip pressure sensors
help the robot adjust how
much force it uses as it learns
to handle a new object.

SUPER SENSORS

Modelled on the human hand, iCub's five jointed fingers offer remarkably lifelike movement. Sensor-packed pads on its fingertips and palm can register tiny changes in force and grip, enabling the robot to manipulate all sorts of objects as it learns about the world through interacting with the objects around it.

MANUFACTURER	ORIGIN	DEVELOPED	HEIGHT	WEIGHT
Hanson Robotics	Hong Kong	2015	85 cm (33 in) for the head and torso	Approximately 18 kg (40 lb)

HUMANOID ROBOT
SOPHIA

Perhaps the most famous humanoid robot, Sophia whips up a media storm wherever it goes, with appearances in television interviews and on fashion magazine covers. More than just a face, this superstar robot can hold a conversation with a human by answering questions, telling jokes, expressing empathy, and ultimately making emotional connections with people. In speeches, it explains how robotics and artificial intelligence will soon become an accepted part of modern-day life. Sophia is also the first robot to be granted citizenship of a country.

The dome at the back of the head houses the main electronics.

The face is made of a special material called "frubber" for its flesh-meets-rubber surface texture.

The facial features were modelled on British actress Audrey Hepburn.

A camera and control panel allow operators to monitor Sophia remotely.

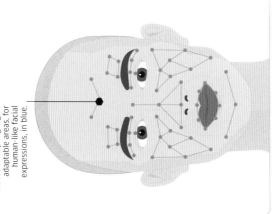

HOW IT WORKS

Artificial intelligence, computer algorithms, and cameras determine Sophia's choice of facial expressions and conversation. First, an image recognition algorithm detects a recognizable face, which triggers another algorithm to supply prewritten possible statements to use. Sophia chooses a phrase to say and awaits a person's first response. A transcription algorithm turns the response into text before this information is analysed for Sophia to choose the best matched option, and the conversation continues.

This facial map highlights adaptable areas, for human-like facial expressions, in blue.

The 3D-printed arms and robotic hands are dexterous enough to perform basic tasks and hold delicate items.

POWER
Power cable, battery

FEATURES
Facial recognition, cameras, and conversation software

The back of Sophia's head is a transparent dome, exposing wires and mechanics. It houses the "brain" or internal processor, which is used for facial recognition, visual data and language processing, speech systems, and motion controls.

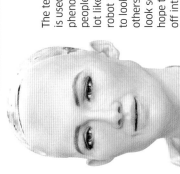

The term "uncanny valley" is used to describe the phenomenon where some people find robots that look a lot like humans creepy. Some robot makers design their bots to look less like humans, but others try to make their bots look so similar to humans in the hope that people will not be put off interacting with them.

ARTIFICIAL INTELLIGENCE

At least ten different versions of Sophia are being worked on by experts around the world to advance its artificial intelligence so any chat flows with the twists and turns of natural conversation, rather than being restricted to specific subjects.

ROBOT RUNAROUND

Help is at hand in hospitals with this healthcare honcho. **RoboCourier** is the go-to delivery service for transporting laboratory specimens, surgical equipment, and patient medication around a hospital. An in-built laser guidance system provides smooth navigation through hospital corridors, while a secure locking container ensures that supplies arrive safely. With staff rushed off their feet, this robot takes the strain.

▲ Three levels of storage allow RoboCourier to multi-task on different deliveries.

ROBOT WORLD

Not too long ago, robots were only created to carry out repetitive or dangerous tasks to save people time and effort. Today, many robots are designed to entertain and enhance our everyday lives with an array of technological talents. Meet the mind-blowing machines ready to share our world.

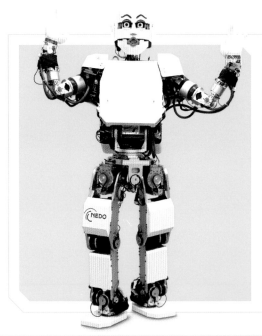

AMUSING ANDROID

Japanese inventors created this humanoid comedian after researching what people find funny. **Kobian** has its own stand-up routine, which uses a mix of exaggerated stories, repetitive gags, and daft impressions. Although some jokes may fall flat, this rib-tickling robot is guaranteed to give you a giggle. Studies have proven that people find their general moods have lifted after watching Kobian perform.

◄ The robot's facial expressions convey seven different "emotions", ranging from joy to disgust.

PROGRAMMED PERFORMER

All the world's a stage for **RoboThespian**. This fully articulated humanoid robot loves performing in front of an audience. Its smooth moves and easy chatter make it the ultimate crowdpleaser at shows, theatres, and exhibitions. RoboThespian can turn teacher, actor, or salesman on cue by choosing one of the preprogrammed settings on a tablet, but its best party trick is telling jokes in 30 different languages.

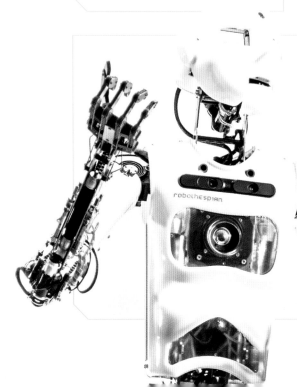

▲ The screens inside RoboThespian's eyes maintain eye contact with people.

ROCK ON, ROBOTS

Made from recycled scrap metal, **Compressorhead** are the heavyweights of heavy metal. These robot rockers line up with a singer, lead guitarist, bassist, and drummer, playing both electric and acoustic instruments. Made in Germany and playing live since 2013, Compressorhead not only play classics – without breaking into a sweat – but have also made their own album called *Party Machine*.

◄ The band consists of drummer Stickboy, lead guitarist Fingers, bassist Bones, second guitarist Helga Ta, and new vocalist Mega-Wattson.

STRING STAR

Let the music play with Toyota's **violin-playing robot**. This humanoid musician hit all the right notes when it played the violin to thrilled audiences. The dexterity of its hands and the joints of its arms allowed the same freedom of movement as in a human violinist. Solo performances were what this first-rate fiddler did best, but similar robots by Toyota can bang the drums and toot the trumpet. The lifelike movements of these musician bots mean they can also perform chores at home.

◄ The violin-playing robot no longer moves and is only on display now.

ROBOT RECEPTION

Don't be alarmed by the unusual front desk of Henn na Hotel in Japan. Here, the check-in process is overseen by **robot receptionists**, including one in the shape of a sharp-clawed dinosaur. This odd hotel has an almost entirely robotic workforce to cut costs and increase efficiency. An automated trolley carries luggage to the rooms, a robot waiter brings room service, and a tank showcases swimming robot fish.

◄ Robot receptionists welcome guests arriving at the hotel.

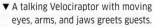

▼ A talking Velociraptor with moving eyes, arms, and jaws greets guests.

MANUFACTURER
ABB

ORIGIN
Switzerland

RELEASED
2015

HEIGHT
56 cm (22 in)

COLLABORATIVE ROBOT
YuMi

This twin-armed bot has conducted orchestras, solved Rubik's Cube puzzles, and even made paper planes, but is most at home on the assembly line. Its fast, deft pair of arms move with incredible accuracy so that it can repeat a task to within just 0.02 mm (0.00079 in) every time, thousands of times. Roughly the same size as the top half of an adult male, YuMi is designed to work closely with humans (its name stands for You and Me, working together), assembling fiddly and delicate smartphones and watches, or putting together and testing complex vehicle parts.

The plastic casing
is soft to the touch.

ROBOT SYMPHONY

In 2017, YuMi became the first robot to conduct an orchestra. It successfully conducted three pieces of classical music at a live performance, with the Lucca Philharmonic Orchestra, in Pisa, Italy. Before the performance, the renowned Italian conductor Andrea Colombini trained YuMi, guiding it through the precise movements that YuMi later mimicked for the music.

WEIGHT
38 kg (83.8 lb)

POWER
Mains
electricity

FEATURES
Cameras with
object-recognition

> **"YuMi allows robots to work hand in hand with human beings."**
>
> *Sam Atiya*, President, **ABB**

The tool flange
can be fitted with
different sizes of
robotic grippers.

Each arm is made of
lightweight magnesium
covered in a plastic
casing. It can reach up
to 56 cm (22 in) in
all directions.

Each joint is powered
by its own electric
motor. Together, they
allow smooth, speedy
movement – up to
1.5 m (4.9 ft)
per second.

TRUMPET PLAYER

Toyota's trumpet-playing Partner robot
wowed audiences with tunes played on
a regular trumpet in 2006. The 1.5-m-
(4.9-ft-) tall humanoid robot used a
pneumatic system to blow air through
the trumpet, and its articulated hand
pushed the trumpet's piston valve
buttons to play different notes.

HOW IT WORKS

A human chef uses the Robotic Kitchen's technology to create a meal. Once the robot has been taught how to make a dish, the data is added to the Robotic Kitchen's database and can be re-used whenever the operator desires.

1 The robot has a 3D camera and wired sensory glove. These turn the human chef's movements into digital instructions that the robot can understand.

2 The robot's two flexible hands are able to use the same utensils that the human chef used. The robot can blend, stir, beat, shake, pour, and drizzle the ingredients.

HOME-HELP ROBOT

ROBOTIC KITCHEN

There's a new chef cooking up a storm in the kitchen. The Moley's Robotic Kitchen is the first fully automated cooking robot, able to copy an expert cook and repeat their movements step by step at the touch of a button. The articulated robotic arms work with the same care and attention as human hands to ensure every dish is delicious. Sit back and let the Robotic Kitchen tickle your tastebuds from a library of mouthwatering recipes.

HANDY WORK

The Moley's Robotic Kitchen has two multi-jointed robot arms with sensor-packed artificial hands, providing the same dexterity and movement as your own hands. It also works at the same speed as the original masterchef who demonstrated the recipe. This human-like motion means the robot is able to use a wide range of cooking appliances and utensils.

MANUFACTURER	ORIGIN	DEVELOPED	HEIGHT	FEATURES
Moley Robotics	UK	2014	Standard kitchen, designed to fit into existing spaces	Tactile sensors and a 3D camera allow replication of human actions with precision

The robotic arms follow the same design as those commonly in use on car production lines.

Each utensil or appliance is used in exactly the same way as the human chef used them.

FUTURE FOOD

Moley's Robotic Kitchen could become a feature in hospitals and care homes, where time is precious but diet is important. Machines like this could lead a robot revolution by allowing people around the world to share or even sell recipes, enjoy international cuisine, and dine on the dishes of celebrated chefs.

MANUFACTURER	ORIGIN	RELEASED	HEIGHT	WEIGHT
Hanson Robotics	Hong Kong	2007	68.6 cm (27 in)	2 kg (4.5 lb)

SOCIAL ROBOT
ZENO

A big star of interactive humanoid robots is Zeno. This cross between a young boy and a cartoon character is known for its flexible face and its range of expressions. This smart bot is also a whizz at reading books, learning foreign languages, and teaching students. But it is not all work and no play. Zeno kicks back in style by telling jokes, playing games, and showing off his dance moves. Thanks to advanced computer software and artificial intelligence, there is no end to his talents.

Freedom of movement in the arms allows for a range of gestures.

TOUCHSCREEN

Zeno's chest contains a touchscreen with multiple options, including educational programmes, university research, games store, general knowledge, and two-way conversation. Children with special needs particularly respond to the robot's compassionate chat and therapy sessions.

An option can be selected by pressing the right part of the touchscreen.

The HD cameras inside the eyes help Zeno recognize and remember different faces.

Zeno communicates through the speakers in its chest.

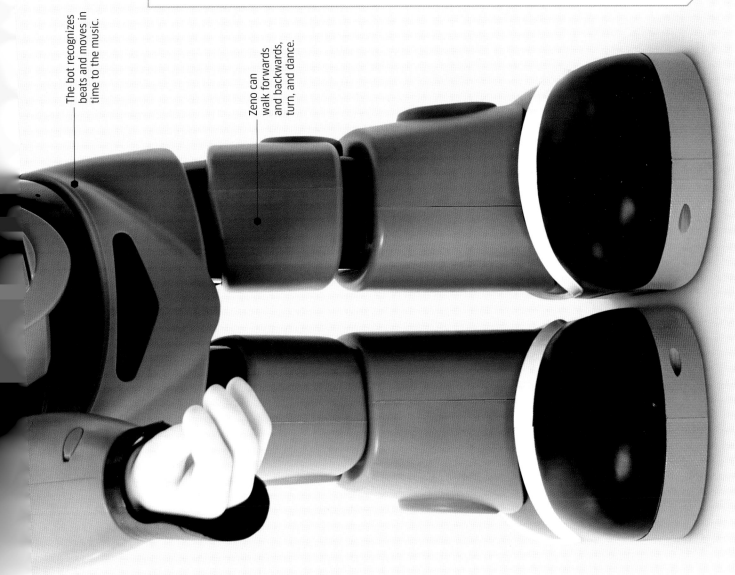

FEATURES
Artificial intelligence, HD cameras, touch sensors, and voice recognition

EXPRESSIVE BOT

Zeno's face is made from frubber, a unique rubbery elastic material used to produce a skin-like effect. Motors in the face instantly mould the frubber into recognizable facial expressions. Zeno's expressions are used to add to the information the robot is trying to display.

SAD

HURT

WORRIED

SURPRISED

HAPPY

TIRED

The bot recognizes beats and moves in time to the music.

Zeno can walk forwards and backwards, turn, and dance.

MANUFACTURER	ORIGIN	DEVELOPED	HEIGHT	WEIGHT
SoftBank Robotics	France	2006	57.3 cm (22.5 in)	5.4 kg (11.9 lb)

HOW IT WORKS

NAO is packed with more than 50 sensors, including sonar for distance measuring. Its sensing unit can detect when the robot is lying down, and its controller can trigger a sequence of movements of its electric motors and joints to get back up. NAO moves its arms back to lever itself up to a sitting upright position before bending its legs to propel itself upright.

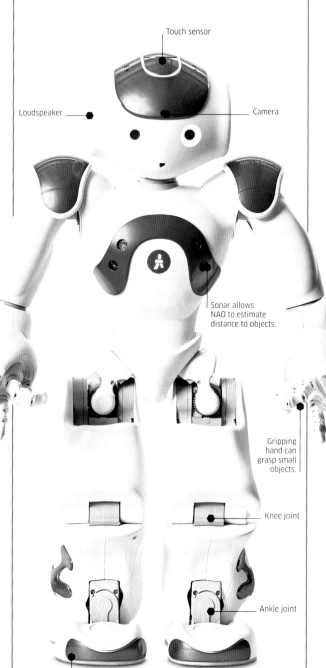

Touch sensor

Loudspeaker

Camera

Sonar allows NAO to estimate distance to objects.

Gripping hand can grasp small objects.

Knee joint

Ankle joint

Foot bumper acts as a sensor for detecting nearby objects.

HUMANOID ROBOT

NAO

Dancing, playing robot soccer, understanding human speech, and entertaining the elderly in care homes – there is no end to this humble humanoid's talents. NAO is versatile enough to be programmed by school students and experienced robotics engineers alike. It is very flexible and its four microphones can recognize voices and obtain instant translations to words in 19 different languages. Its balance sensors help the robot stay on its feet as it walks, but if it does fall over, NAO knows how to get back on its feet all by itself.

VISION

NAO has two cameras, but they aren't in its eyes. One camera sits on its forehead, with the other in its "mouth". NAO's eyes are instead used to help it communicate with humans by changing colour.

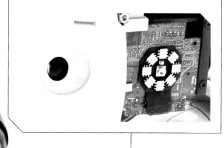

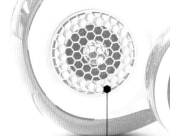

The loudspeaker can broadcast information from the internet.

POWER
Battery

FEATURES
Can detect faces and objects,
and recognize speech

AMAZING AVATAR

Kids with injuries or illnesses often
miss out on a lot of school. One of
NAO's capabilities is to act as the
absent child's avatar – a representation
of them in one place when they are
somewhere else. A child can use a
tablet to control NAO from afar, getting
the robot to collect information, video,
or sound from the classroom, and send
it back to the child.

Three buttons on
the head can be
programmed to wake
NAO up, or perform
an action.

SMOOTH MOVES
The small humanoid robot NAO has wowed many with its ability to dance. More than 10,000 of these smart, fluid movers have been built. Many of them have been programmed to perform complex dance routines on their own or with other NAO robots, staying perfectly in sync by communicating wirelessly.

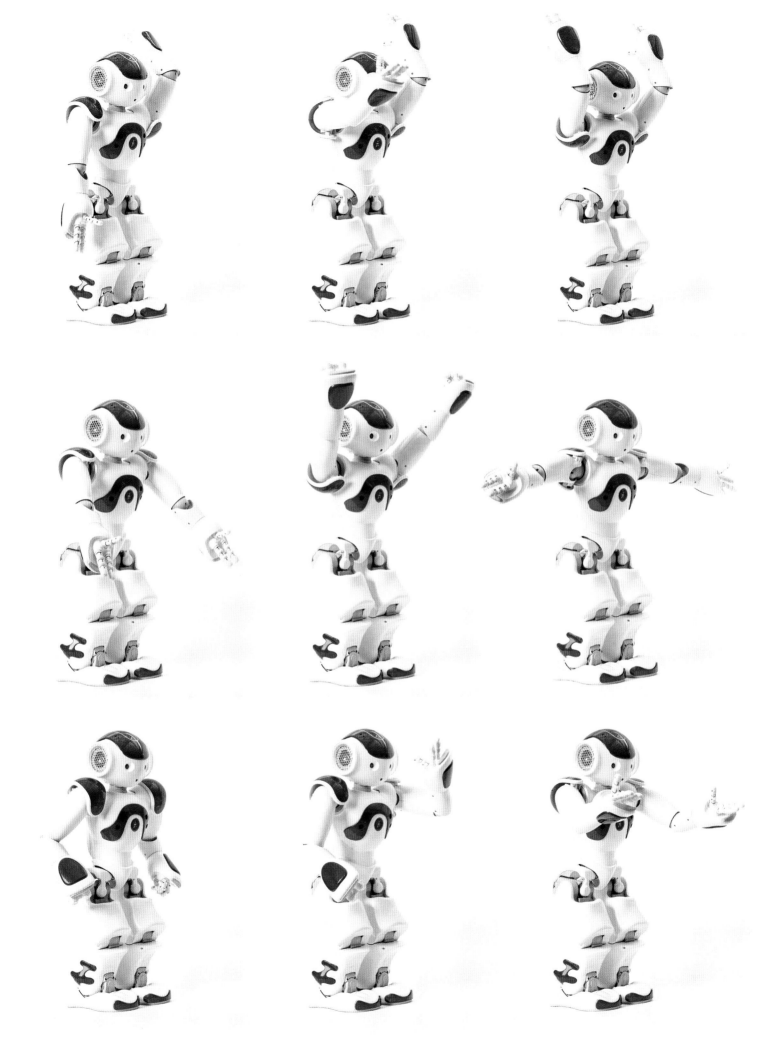

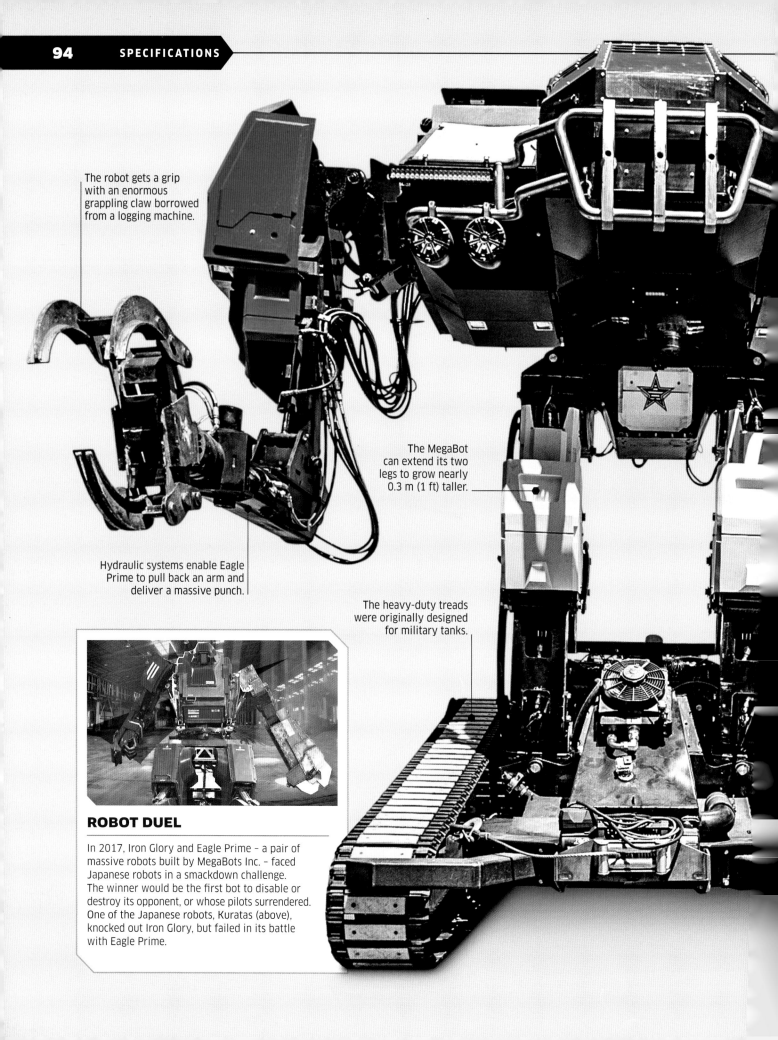

The robot gets a grip with an enormous grappling claw borrowed from a logging machine.

The MegaBot can extend its two legs to grow nearly 0.3 m (1 ft) taller.

Hydraulic systems enable Eagle Prime to pull back an arm and deliver a massive punch.

The heavy-duty treads were originally designed for military tanks.

ROBOT DUEL

In 2017, Iron Glory and Eagle Prime – a pair of massive robots built by MegaBots Inc. – faced Japanese robots in a smackdown challenge. The winner would be the first bot to disable or destroy its opponent, or whose pilots surrendered. One of the Japanese robots, Kuratas (above), knocked out Iron Glory, but failed in its battle with Eagle Prime.

MANUFACTURER	ORIGIN	DEVELOPED	HEIGHT	WEIGHT	POWER
MegaBots Inc.	USA	2015	4.9 m (16 ft)	13 tonnes	Gasoline-powered engine

The working parts are covered with an armour of tough, protective steel.

HOW IT WORKS

The "guts" of the Eagle Prime MegaBot contain more than 1.6 km (1 mile) of cabling. There are more than 650 cables and 300 electronic devices inside this hulking machine. Each pilot manipulates a complex array of joysticks, pedals, and more than 40 toggle switches to control and move the bot. A booming gasoline-powered engine and a transmission taken from a boat keep the MegaBot moving. When fully operational, the bot is strong enough to lift and crush a car in the air.

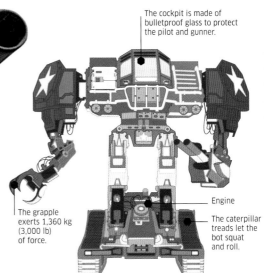

The cockpit is made of bulletproof glass to protect the pilot and gunner.

The grapple exerts 1,360 kg (3,000 lb) of force.

Engine

The caterpillar treads let the bot squat and roll.

The double-barrelled cannon shoots powerful paintballs heavy enough to shatter glass.

PILOTED ROBOT

MegaBots

The engineers behind MegaBots are making the stuff of science fiction a reality – a giant fighting robot battling another mechanical monster in an epic sporting combat. MegaBots are operated by a pilot and a gunner sitting inside a protective glass cockpit atop the bot. Complex control panels inside allow them to control the robot and its formidable weapons. An array of HD cameras give them an amazing overview of the battle.

MANUFACTURER
Intelligent
System Corporation

ORIGIN
Japan

RELEASED
2001

HEIGHT
57 cm (22 in)

WEIGHT
2.7 kg (6 lb)

SOCIAL ROBOT
PARO

PARO is a super-soft robotic seal designed for use in hospitals and nursing homes as a robotic form of pet therapy. Pets have been shown to help the emotional, social, and even cognitive (brain) functioning of patients with certain illnesses, but sometimes patients lack the ability to properly care for a real animal. PARO is modelled on a baby harp seal's appearance and behaviour, while swapping blubber for batteries. More than 1,300 PARO robots are already hard at work in Japan, with others being introduced to Europe and the USA. Simply irresistible, the friendly fuzzball is one of the world's most commonly used therapeutic robots.

Artificial anti-bacterial fur is soft but strong, and also resistant to dirt and damage.

Head moves in different directions to follow sounds.

Big, beautiful eyes blink regularly and close during petting.

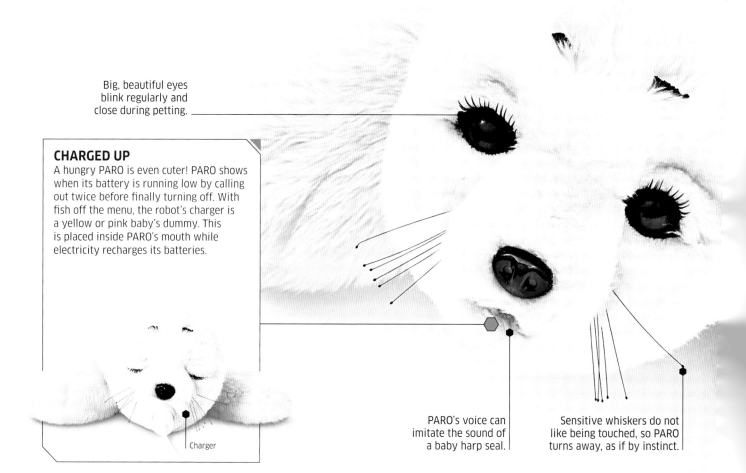

CHARGED UP
A hungry PARO is even cuter! PARO shows when its battery is running low by calling out twice before finally turning off. With fish off the menu, the robot's charger is a yellow or pink baby's dummy. This is placed inside PARO's mouth while electricity recharges its batteries.

Charger

PARO's voice can imitate the sound of a baby harp seal.

Sensitive whiskers do not like being touched, so PARO turns away, as if by instinct.

97

POWER
Internal
rechargeable battery

FEATURES
Microphones,
motors, and sensors

SET THE SEAL

PARO's job is patient care, particularly for elderly people suffering with memory loss. The enthusiastic way in which PARO responds to gentle touch has been proven to reduce patient stress and create a calmer atmosphere. It is also programmed to remember previous responses and adapt its personality to please the patient by repeating positive patterns of behaviour.

> **❝**Just like animals used in **pet therapy**, PARO can help relieve depression and anxiety – but it never needs to be fed... **❞**
>
> *Takanori Shibata,* Designer, **PARO**

Twelve sensors embedded in the fur react to touch.

Feelings are shown by facial expressions, body movements, and sounds.

RELIABLE RUNNER

Another home-helping robot is HOBBIT. This mobility assistance bot makes life easier by performing jobs that can be challenging for elderly or disabled people. The makers of HOBBIT wanted to foster a relationship of mutual care between the robot and humans, similar to how a bond is built between a pet and its owner. The robot can tidy trip hazards away from floors, play games with its owner, and sound an alarm in emergency situations.

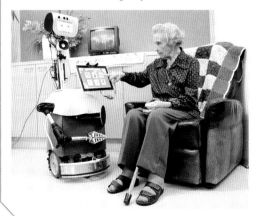

PARO can lift its flippers like a real seal, thanks to motors inside it.

MANUFACTURER Festo	**ORIGIN** Germany	**DEVELOPED** 2013	**LENGTH** 44 cm (17 in)

BIOMIMETIC ROBOT

BionicOpter

Dragonflies are among the fastest and most manoeuvrable insects in the animal kingdom. At 44 cm (17 in) long and with a whopping 63 cm (2 ft) wingspan, this dragonfly drone – called the BionicOpter – is much bigger than real dragonflies, and almost as quick. This robot can continually adjust the performance of its fast-beating wings and the position of its head and tail during flight. As a result, it can switch from climbing to diving, swoop left or right, or hover in mid-air smoothly. It can even fly backwards, just like a real dragonfly.

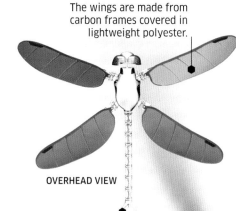

The wings are made from carbon frames covered in lightweight polyester.

OVERHEAD VIEW

The tail can move up or down to steer the robot.

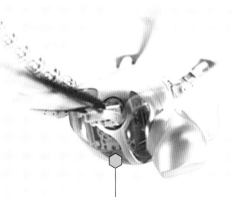

IN CONTROL

The motors, which turn lightweight gears, are instructed by the robot's microcontroller, which coordinates all the different actions required for the robot to fly. This leaves the user to simply choose flight direction or destination using an app.

The bot's head and eyes are sculpted to look like a large dragonfly, but BionicOpter has no cameras and cannot "see".

WEIGHT
175 g (0.38 lb)

POWER
Battery

FEATURES
Coordinates complex
actions to produce
smooth movement

SHAPE CHANGER

A special type of metal alloy, called nitinol, is used as a form of muscle in BionicOpter's tail. When an electric current is passed through it, the nitinol warms up and shrinks in size, pulling the tail either up or down.

The four wings can beat at 15–20 strokes per second.

The body covering is made of lightweight and flexible materials.

BionicOpter's ribcage is packed with twin batteries, a microcontroller, and nine different motors.

HOW IT WORKS

The robot's microcontroller constantly monitors and adjusts the wings. A main motor in the body can vary the speed of the up and down movement of the wings. Two tiny motors in each wing alter how deeply it moves on each stroke. The wings can also be twisted up to 90° from a horizontal position to alter the direction of the wings' thrust. The movable head and tail add further ways to help steer.

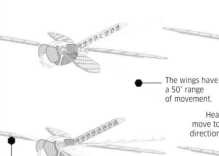

The wings have a 50° range of movement.

Individual wings can be twisted by 90°.

Head and tail move to alter the direction of flight.

Motors control the depth of each stroke.

MANUFACTURER
Faraday Future

ORIGIN
USA

DEVELOPED
2016

PILOTED ROBOT

FFZERO1

This stunning, sleek, single-seat racer is packed full of the latest tech – from smartphone control of aspects of the vehicle's performance such as level of grip and ride height, to using batteries instead of fuel to power the car. The FFZERO1 is a concept car, acting as a showcase for new advances and technologies, some borrowed from robotics and electronics. Most fascinating of all is its potential to be fitted with sensors and controllers to make it a self-driving vehicle, which might be able to take control on a racing track and guide a driver around, showing them the quickest racing line.

HOW IT WORKS

Driverless cars rely on many different sensors, which work with high-resolution digital maps to navigate and drive safely. A driverless car's sensors sweep its immediate surroundings to provide real-time tracking of other vehicles and pedestrians, and the directions and speeds they are moving at. Cameras capture a 360° view around the vehicle, which is analysed by object recognition software to spot other vehicles, traffic lights, stop signals, and other road signs. The car's controller continually instructs the vehicle's motors to change speed, alter direction, or to stop, depending on the information it receives.

The transparent tailfin improves aerodynamics.

HIGH PERFORMANCE

The FFZERO1's high performance batteries are linked together in the floor of the vehicle to give it a hefty 8-10 times the power of a small hatchback car. This, in turn, gives this fast vehicle a startling acceleration. It can travel from a stationary position to 96 km/h (60 mph) in under three seconds.

Bus

A driverless car's cameras and sensors track a bus going past at a junction. The car slows down to obey a stop sign it has spotted.

SMART COCKPIT

The driver sits cocooned in the centre of the car, protected by a band called a halo. A smartphone can be clipped into the steering wheel to control some aspects of the vehicle's performance, and to visualize the track and other data on its screen.

A smartphone sits inside the steering wheel.

The glass roof has hinges at the back to open up for the driver to enter and exit the vehicle.

The sculpted body shell is made of strong but lightweight carbon fibre.

The lightweight alloy wheel is turned by its own dedicated electric motor.

Multiple air tunnels channel airflow along the length of the car, reducing drag and cooling the vehicle's electric motors. In addition, the air tunnels help increase downforce, giving the car more grip.

GOING TO EXTREMES

The solutions to many robotics questions are to be found in the natural world. Roboticists are increasingly studying animals to find new ways of completing tasks. As a result, robots are going into places they have never gone before – from underwater robotic eels to robots that work together like bees.

MANUFACTURER
Stanford University

ORIGIN
USA

RELEASED
2016

HEIGHT
1.5 m (4.9 ft)

POWER
Lithium-ion battery,
electric tether

WORK ROBOT

OceanOne

Robot submersibles have been at work for years, but OceanOne is really making big waves. This bot was developed to use the experience of a skilled human diver, while avoiding many of the dangers humans face underwater. OceanOne has stereoscopic vision to enable its pilot to see exactly what the robot sees in high definition. Its arms and hands are controlled by joysticks and it can grasp delicate objects without damaging them, allowing the bot to perform highly skilled tasks in dangerous conditions. Eventually, it will dive alongside humans, communicating with them as they explore together.

The arms can keep the bot's hands steady even if the body is moving.

The cables provide power as well as the signal and mechanical links between OceanOne and its controllers.

HOW IT WORKS

OceanOne is shaped like a human diver, making it an avatar of its operator. The upper body holds the cameras, two articulated (flexible) arms, and a pair of hands packed with force sensors. The robot's batteries, on-board computers, and power thrusters are found in the lower part.

Eight multi-directional thrusters move the bot through the water.

Battery

Wrist

The on-board electronics are immersed in oil instead of being waterproofed.

The head houses stereoscopic cameras.

Forearm

Rigid foam

Elbow

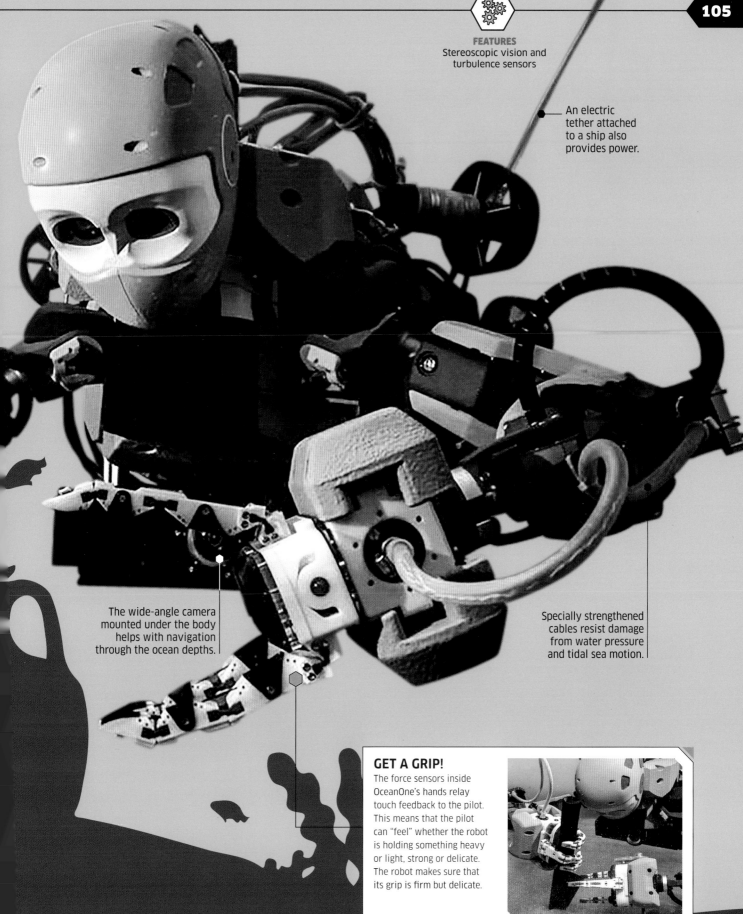

An electric
tether attached
to a ship also
provides power.

The wide-angle camera
mounted under the body
helps with navigation
through the ocean depths.

Specially strengthened
cables resist damage
from water pressure
and tidal sea motion.

GET A GRIP!

The force sensors inside
OceanOne's hands relay
touch feedback to the pilot.
This means that the pilot
can "feel" whether the robot
is holding something heavy
or light, strong or delicate.
The robot makes sure that
its grip is firm but delicate.

SENSORS AND DATA

Robots rely on sensors to acquire information about the world around them. They also need data about themselves and the position and functioning of their various parts. Sensors come in many forms. Some sensors, such as cameras or microphones, mimic human senses. Others give robots data-gathering abilities that humans lack, such as identifying tiny traces of a particular chemical or detecting distances accurately in total darkness.

Sensing acceleration and tilt

Accelerometers are sensors that measure acceleration – the change in speed of an object. They are used in robotics not only to sense changes in motion, but also to help robots measure tilt and angles and to keep their balance.

Piezoelectric accelerometer

This type of sensor features a weight (called the mass) on a spring and a small piezoelectric crystal connected to an electric circuit.

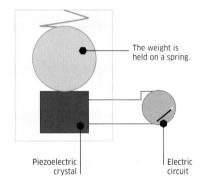

The weight is held on a spring.

Piezoelectric crystal

Electric circuit

Sensing danger

Sensors can be the difference between success or failure for robots deployed in remote regions far away from their human operators. Some sensors alert the robot of impending problems or dangers if the robot continues to perform its work. Radiation sensors, for instance, can warn a robot that a highly radioactive source is near that could damage or even destroy the robot's circuits.

Sensing metal

An inductive proximity sensor can detect metal nearby before the robot comes into contact with it. This could be critical in the case of a robot in an area containing landmines.

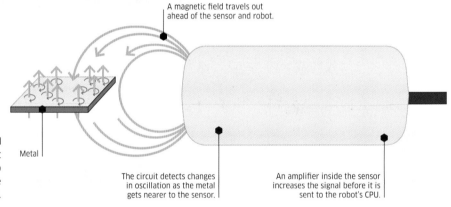

A magnetic field travels out ahead of the sensor and robot.

Metal

The circuit detects changes in oscillation as the metal gets nearer to the sensor.

An amplifier inside the sensor increases the signal before it is sent to the robot's CPU.

Different ways of seeing

Human eyes see a particular range of light, but robot sensors are able to see more. These include thermal imaging sensors that can see things by the heat they emit, or sensors that use lasers, radar, or sonar to build up a 3D picture of the environment around a robot.

Rotating LiDAR sensor emits and collects pulses of light to measure distances.

Combining sensors

Driverless cars use cameras to spot traffic signs and LiDAR to create a 360° image of the car's surroundings. Radar and other sensors track vehicles and other moving objects.

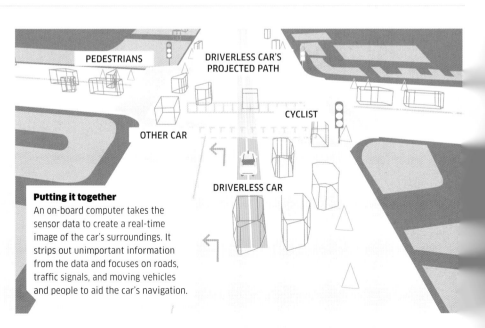

PEDESTRIANS

DRIVERLESS CAR'S PROJECTED PATH

CYCLIST

OTHER CAR

DRIVERLESS CAR

Putting it together

An on-board computer takes the sensor data to create a real-time image of the car's surroundings. It strips out unimportant information from the data and focuses on roads, traffic signals, and moving vehicles and people to aid the car's navigation.

Accelerometers are constructed in a number of different ways. Many use piezoelectricity – the property of some materials to give out an electric voltage when they are squeezed or compressed.

Acceleration

An acceration force pushes the weight down onto the crystal. This compresses the crystal, which causes it to produces an electric voltage that is measured to find the acceleration rate.

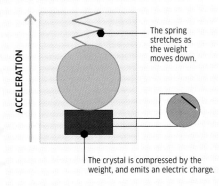

ACCELERATION

The spring stretches as the weight moves down.

The crystal is compressed by the weight, and emits an electric charge.

AIR PRESSURE

HUMIDITY

WIND SPEED

HEAT   **POLLUTION**

Environmental sensors

Wind gauges, thermometers, pollution sensors, and other environmental sensors allow robots to measure their surroundings. This data may be of scientific interest or, in the case of detecting severe heat, to protect the robot itself.

Underwater sensing

Fish and some amphibians have a fascinating extra sense: the ability to detect changes in water pressure and flow caused by other moving creatures, or water flowing around static objects nearby. This is their lateral-line sense, and it allows fish to detect prey or predators nearby. Tiny electrical parts called thermistors have been used to give some robots this sense. A thermistor features a microscopic heated wire that changes temperature when the flow of water changes. The lateral-line sense may give robots a way of understanding environment in poor visibility.

Snookie

This underwater robot was built by researchers in Germany. Its nose contains an artificial lateral-line sensor that helps the robot to detect obstacles.

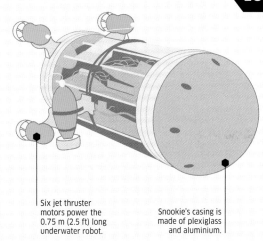

Six jet thruster motors power the 0.75 m (2.5 ft) long underwater robot.

Snookie's casing is made of plexiglass and aluminium.

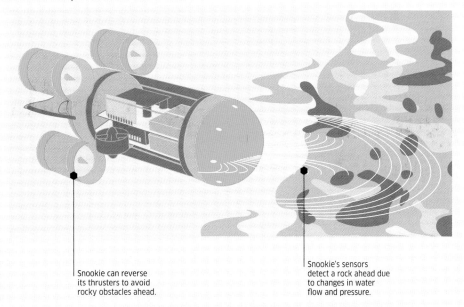

Snookie can reverse its thrusters to avoid rocky obstacles ahead.

Snookie's sensors detect a rock ahead due to changes in water flow and pressure.

Future driverless cars

In future, the sensors used by driverless cars will create faster, more detailed "vision" by using 4D cameras. These take wide-angle images which are packed with other information including the direction and distance of all the light that reaches the camera's lens from objects.

A 4D camera image covers an angle of 138° – more than a third of a circle.

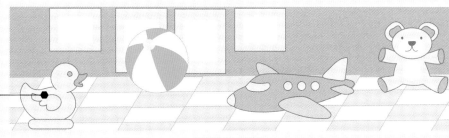

ORIGINAL SCENE

The image is processed to include data on the distances of objects from the camera (the blue areas are closer and white further away).

4D CAMERA

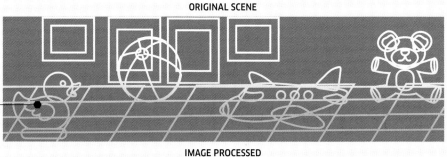

IMAGE PROCESSED

MANUFACTURER	ORIGIN	DEVELOPED	HEIGHT	WEIGHT
Festo	Germany	2015	4.3 cm (1.7 in)	105 g (0.23 lb)

SWARM ROBOT
BionicANTs

This six-legged scuttler is the size of your hand and crammed full of technology. The BionicANT's movement is guided by stereo cameras, first used by MAVs (micro aerial vehicles), and an optical floor sensor originally from a computer mouse. Much of the rest of each BionicANT, though, is innovative – from its low-power system for movement to how the autonomous ants work together to solve a problem, sharing data over a wireless network. Technologies tested on the BionicANTs may lead to more productive factories as well as robust robots that can explore tough terrain.

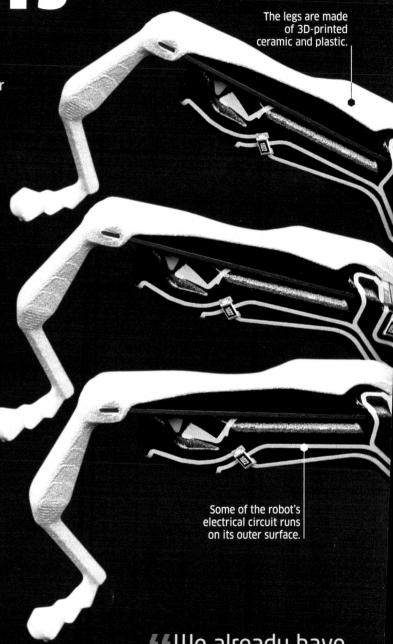

The legs are made of 3D-printed ceramic and plastic.

Some of the robot's electrical circuit runs on its outer surface.

HOW THEY WORK

The robot's leg and gripper movement come from tiny, power-thrifty devices called piezoelectric transducers. These bend when they receive an electric current. Each leg has three transducers so that it can lift, or move backwards or forwards to take 1-cm (0.4-in) steps. The robot's processor acts as its controller. It synchronizes all the signals and the electric current sent to the transducers to coordinate the legs' movement.

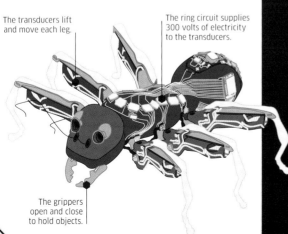

The transducers lift and move each leg.

The ring circuit supplies 300 volts of electricity to the transducers.

The grippers open and close to hold objects.

"We already have autonomous devices but they get more and more intelligent and more functional."

Elias Knubben, Head of Bionic Projects, Festo

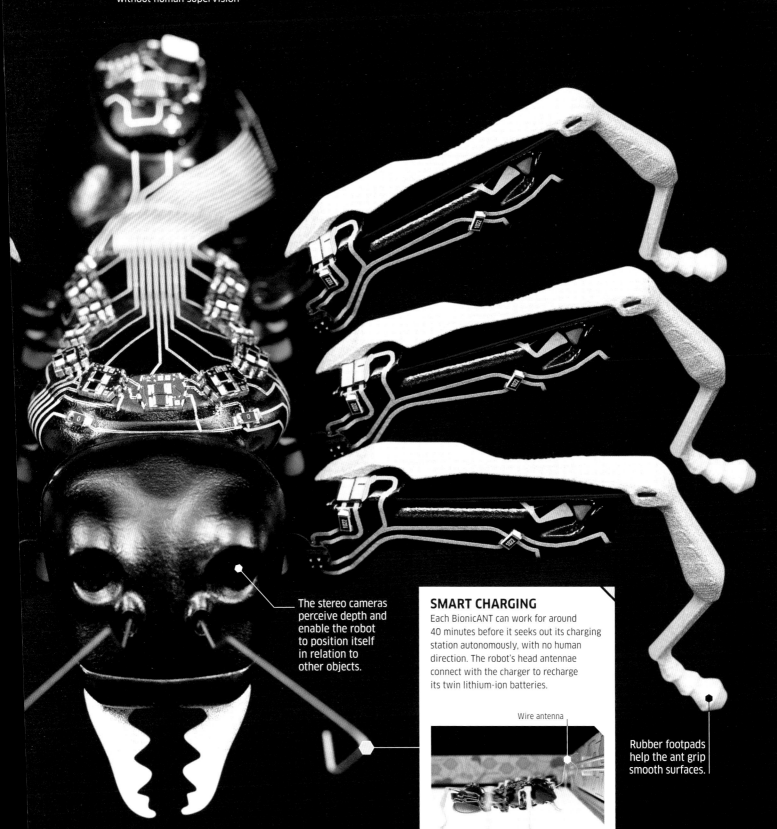

POWER
Battery

FEATURES
Works with other robots
without human supervision

The stereo cameras
perceive depth and
enable the robot
to position itself
in relation to
other objects.

SMART CHARGING

Each BionicANT can work for around
40 minutes before it seeks out its charging
station autonomously, with no human
direction. The robot's head antennae
connect with the charger to recharge
its twin lithium-ion batteries.

Wire antenna

Rubber footpads
help the ant grip
smooth surfaces.

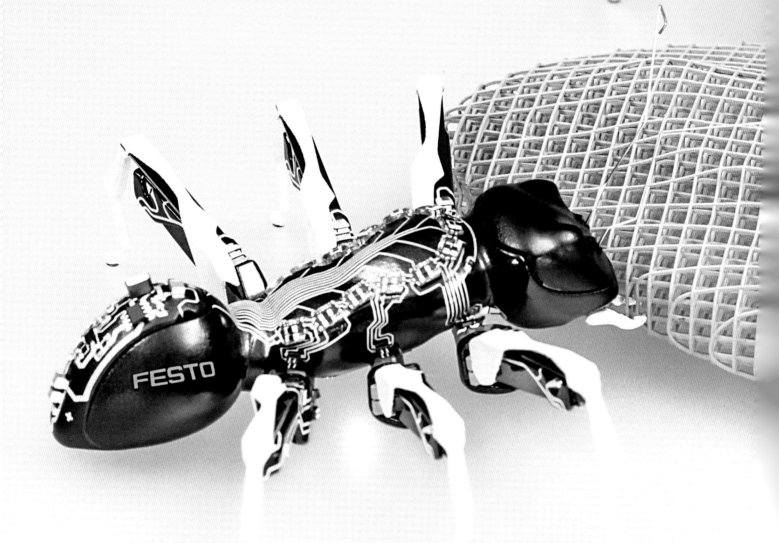

COLLABORATIVE WORKERS

This is no three-way battle. It's actually a group of extraordinary BionicANTs working together to move a large load between them. Based on the teamwork exhibited by real-life ants, these 3D-printed robot insects constantly share information by using radio signals sent and received from electronics in their abdomens. Similar collaborative robots could play major roles in search and rescue missions and exploration in future.

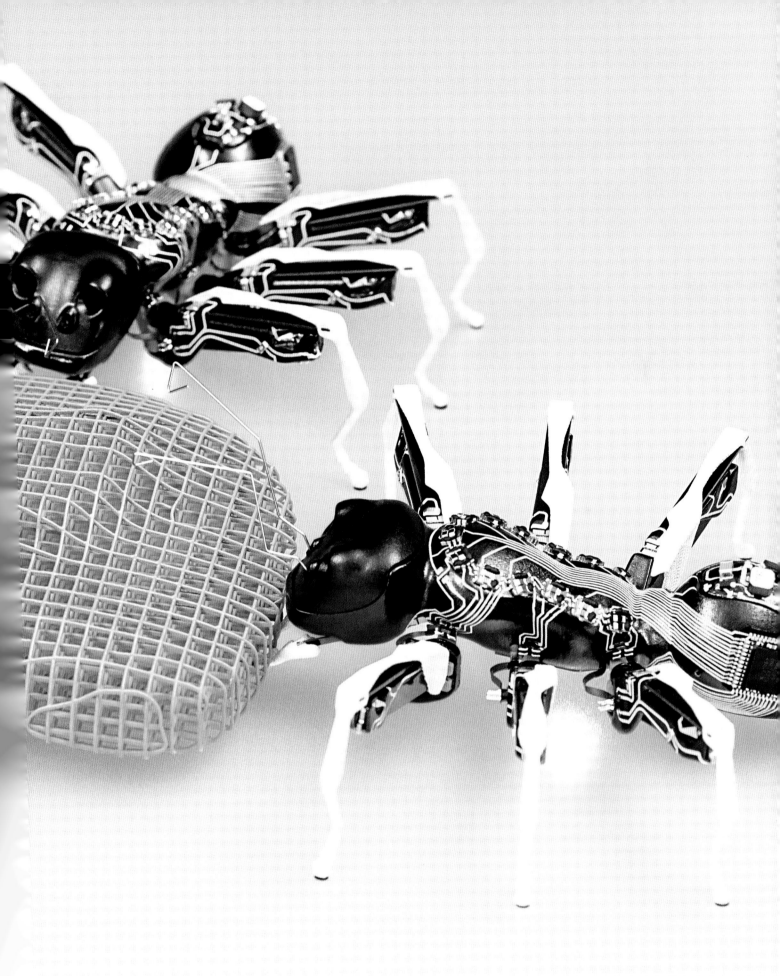

MANUFACTURER
Harvard University

ORIGIN
USA

DEVELOPED
2016

SIZE
6.5 cm
(2.5 in) long

POWER
Fuelled by
hydrogen peroxide

MAKING THE MACHINE

A combination of 3D printing, moulding, and soft lithography (a type of printing technique) is used to manufacture Octobot in a simple, quick, and repeatable process. The bot's "brain" is a fluid-based circuit placed inside an octopus-shaped mould, before a silicone mixture is poured on top. Next, a 3D printer injects platinum ink into the silicone. The complete mould is heated for about four days until the bot's body is ready.

The platinum ink injected into Octobot glows in the dark.

A tiny reservoir holds the liquid hydrogen peroxide.

BIOMIMETIC ROBOT

OCTOBOT

An octopus has no skeleton, and, similarly, there is no tough technology in Octobot's tiny tentacles. Octobot is the world's first completely soft, autonomous robot. Forget batteries, microchips, and computer control. Instead, this bot is 3D printed using soft silicone, and powered by a chemical reaction. It took a team from Harvard University, USA, more than 300 attempts to successfully create Octobot, using a fluid-filled circuit flowing through its silicone body. In future, similar soft bots could be used for sea rescue and military surveillance, as they can fit into narrow spaces and mould into their environment.

HOW IT WORKS

Octobot is powered by a chemical reaction. A tiny amount of liquid hydrogen peroxide pumped inside Octobot pushes through the tubes until it comes into contact with platinum and turns into gas. This chemical reaction causes the tentacles to inflate, which moves the bot through water. Octobot's creators plan to add sensors to it so it can navigate on its own.

1 Thin tubes feed coloured hydrogen peroxide into Octobot.

2 As the chemicals inside the body react, Octobot's tentacles move.

3 Octobot can run for eight minutes on 1 ml (0.03 fl oz) of fuel.

The colours represent the pathways taken by the hydrogen peroxide fuel.

The silicone rubber body fits easily into the palm of your hand.

EDIBLE ACTUATOR

Soft robotics also includes making certain parts of regular robots edible. Scientists in Switzerland have been working on making a digestible robot actuator (a part that makes something else move). If actuators were safe to digest, they could be placed on tiny, edible robots and swallowed by humans or animals. Digestible robots could explore our bodies to scan our insides closely, or assist with medical procedures.

Ingestible parts

STRONG AND STABLE

A front-runner among humanoid robots, **Atlas** can make sophisticated movements of its arms, body, and legs. Its hands can lift and grab objects, while its feet stay upright on tough terrain. The battery-powered hardware is partly 3D printed to create a lightweight compact robot with stereo vision and sensors.

MICRO BOTS

These micro-robots are built using miniature printed circuit boards and magnets. Thousands of them working together like a factory assembly line can manufacture large-scale products. Micro-robots like **MicroFactory** could revolutionize the future of medicine by entering and exploring the body to test and improve human and animal health.

▶ A collection of micro-robots can perform a variety of tasks, including carrying parts, depositing liquids, and building fixed structures.

EXTREME BOTS

Even the trickiest terrain is no problem for these all-action technological trailblazers which push the boundaries of exploration. These remotely controlled robots help humans achieve their goals and stop at nothing to get the job done – whether they are battling germs inside the human body, adventuring into unknown territories, diving into the oceans, or even soaring into space.

EXPLORING TITAN

NASA's **Dragonfly** is a proposed spacecraft that will be able to take off and land repeatedly on Titan, the planet Saturn's largest moon. Using multiple rotors, Dragonfly is expected to take off in 2024 to explore the dense atmosphere and methane lakes of Titan, as well as take samples from the surface to look for possible signs of life. This would be the second craft ever to reach Titan, after NASA's *Huygens* probe which landed there in 2005.

▶ Dragonfly will drop down at regular landing sites on Titan, using its suite of scientific instruments for investigation.

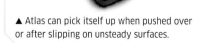

▲ Atlas can pick itself up when pushed over or after slipping on unsteady surfaces.

DEEP-WATER SUBMARINE

Robot submarines, such as **NOC robots**, are leading scientific research in oceans around the world. These long-range autonomous underwater vehicles (AUVs) can now dive under water as well as under ice, reaching depths of 6,000 m (19,700 ft). These robots are preprogrammed with set tasks, and the information they discover is transmitted via a radio link to scientists on board ships or on land.

Most AUVs are shaped like torpedos.

◄ Deployed from ships, AUVs can stay underwater for months at a time.

UNDERWATER GUARDIAN

This marine robot is on a mission to protect coral reefs from increasing numbers of lionfish. Covered in venomous spines, the lionfish reproduces rapidly, reducing fish stocks and destroying coral reefs in the process. Diving to 120 m (400 ft), **Guardian LF1** stuns the lionfish with electric currents and sucks them inside a container.

▼ The Guardian LF1 robot can reach depths unsafe for humans.

▲ The 100-m-(328-ft-) long tether is attached to a controller on the surface.

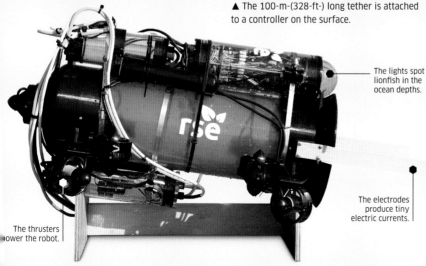

The lights spot lionfish in the ocean depths.

The electrodes produce tiny electric currents.

The thrusters power the robot.

GROWING BOT

A new soft bot that can grow by spreading in one direction without even moving its body, **vinebot's** design was influenced by natural organisms, such as vines and fungi, that grow by spreading out. When put through its paces by an experimental design team, the flexible vinebot could cross a tricky obstacle course and navigate steep walls, long pipes, and tight spaces. Experts hope that in future vinebot can be used for medical devices as well as search and rescue operations.

▲ A lightweight soft tube, vinebot can move towards a set location or grow into its own structure.

MANUFACTURER
Festo

> **"The eMotionButterflies are fully manoeuvrable, very agile and come extremely close to their biological role model."**
>
> **Festo**

Wings are made of a frame of curved carbon rods covered with a thin and lightweight capacitor film, a material that stores electric charge.

ELECTRONIC UNIT

The butterfly's electronics include a microcontroller, compass, accelerometer, gyroscope, and two infrared LED lights. These are all powered by a pair of batteries, which can be recharged in just 15 minutes. All of this is stored in a lightweight package that mimics nature. Each butterfly bot weighs just 32 g (0.07 lb) – about a third of the weight of a deck of playing cards.

The butterfly has a wingspan of 50 cm (19.7 in).

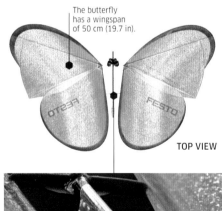

TOP VIEW

SWARM ROBOT

eMotion Butterflies

Beautiful robotic butterflies, with wingspans of half a metre all flutter close to each other in a tight space. How do they do this without colliding? The secret is in how they are controlled from afar, using infrared cameras linked to a powerful central computer. The butterflies themselves are amazing feats of engineering, cramming in a microprocessor, sensors, and twin motors that beat their wings. Powerful batteries may allow this sort of technology to lead to flying robot flocks or swarms that can monitor remote pipelines and structures.

ORIGIN
Germany

POWER
Battery

FEATURES
Collective "swarm"
intelligence

117

On-board electronics adjust each wing's flapping speed and turning point to enable the robot to move through the air.

Wings beat up to two times every second, giving the butterfly bot a top speed of 2.5 m per second (8 ft per second).

HOW THEY WORK

Ten high-speed infrared cameras map the area in which the robots fly. They track each butterfly's infrared LEDs, which act as markers. The constant stream of data is sent to a central computer, which works like air traffic control at an airport. It has the considerable task of analysing 3.7 billion pixels per second to update the position of each butterfly. If a butterfly deviates from its expected flight path, the computer sends instructions to the robot to correct this.

Each infrared camera captures 160 images per second. They're placed so that each butterfly bot is recorded by at least two cameras at all times.

The butterfly robots are instructed by radio signals from the central computer. Each robot is given its own flight path to travel safely.

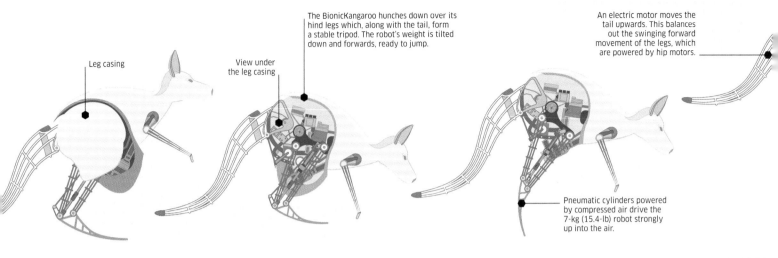

The BionicKangaroo hunches down over its hind legs which, along with the tail, form a stable tripod. The robot's weight is tilted down and forwards, ready to jump.

An electric motor moves the tail upwards. This balances out the swinging forward movement of the legs, which are powered by hip motors.

Leg casing

View under the leg casing

Pneumatic cylinders powered by compressed air drive the 7-kg (15.4-lb) robot strongly up into the air.

Slithering

Some snakebots move by curling and uncurling their long, flexible bodies the way real snakes do. For example, to move forwards, a snake might pull its body up in a series of curves and then thrust it forwards, uncurling as it goes, in a concertina motion. A sidewinder motion (see below) enables a segmented snakebot to climb up uneven terrain.

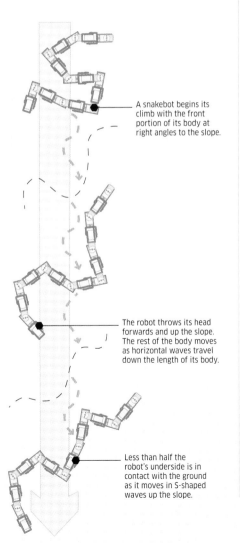

A snakebot begins its climb with the front portion of its body at right angles to the slope.

The robot throws its head forwards and up the slope. The rest of the body moves as horizontal waves travel down the length of its body.

Less than half the robot's underside is in contact with the ground as it moves in S-shaped waves up the slope.

UNUSUAL MOVES

Legs, wheels, and tracks are not the only ways robots can move. In the search for more efficient methods of robot locomotion, robotics engineers have considered unusual ways of propelling their robots so they can keep their balance, overcome obstacles, and operate in difficult locations. Some engineers have looked to nature for inspiration, building robots that mimic the movement patterns of particular creatures.

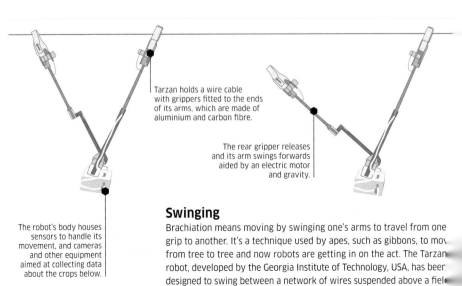

Tarzan holds a wire cable with grippers fitted to the ends of its arms, which are made of aluminium and carbon fibre.

The rear gripper releases and its arm swings forwards aided by an electric motor and gravity.

The robot's body houses sensors to handle its movement, and cameras and other equipment aimed at collecting data about the crops below.

Swinging

Brachiation means moving by swinging one's arms to travel from one grip to another. It's a technique used by apes, such as gibbons, to move from tree to tree and now robots are getting in on the act. The Tarzan robot, developed by the Georgia Institute of Technology, USA, has been designed to swing between a network of wires suspended above a field on a farm, to examine crops without damaging them.

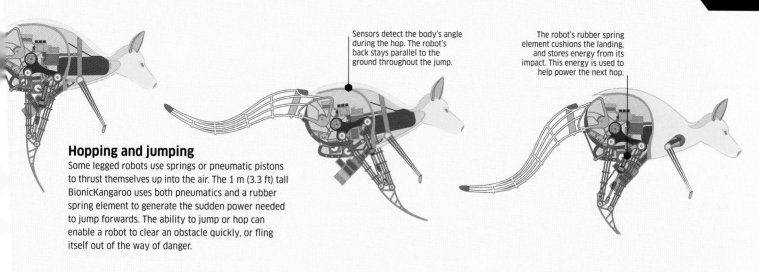

Hopping and jumping

Some legged robots use springs or pneumatic pistons to thrust themselves up into the air. The 1 m (3.3 ft) tall BionicKangaroo uses both pneumatics and a rubber spring element to generate the sudden power needed to jump forwards. The ability to jump or hop can enable a robot to clear an obstacle quickly, or fling itself out of the way of danger.

Sensors detect the body's angle during the hop. The robot's back stays parallel to the ground throughout the jump.

The robot's rubber spring element cushions the landing, and stores energy from its impact. This energy is used to help power the next hop.

The circular frames that house the propellers tilt to face the wall. The thrust they generate keeps the robot's wheels pressing against the wall's surface.

The 3D-printed front wheels are steerable, enabling the robot to turn while travelling on the wall.

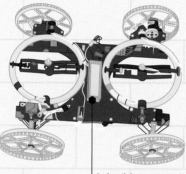

An inertial measurement unit fitted to the robot's carbon fibre baseplate judges whether the robot is on the ground and horizontal or vertically climbing a wall.

Moving vertically

Moving up walls and across ceilings can be a useful skill for robots designed to work in exploration or in danger zones. Some legged robots have been fitted with suction grippers powered by pneumatics to cling onto walls. Other prototype bots have a similar solution to the adhesive hairs of geckos, which provide a sticky grip on vertical surfaces. Another ingenious locomotion system uses propellers in circular frames that can change their angle to generate the thrust needed to keep the robot travelling against gravity.

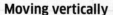

The other arm anchors the robot to the wire.

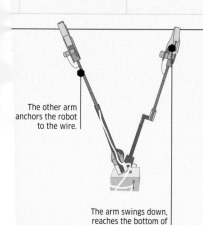

The arm swings down, reaches the bottom of its arc, and then travels back up again.

The rear propeller spins, pushing air back and propelling the robot forwards towards the wall.

The front propeller is angled to thrust the front wheels of the robot up the wall.

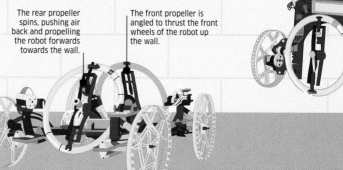

MANUFACTURER
Eelume AS

ORIGIN
Norway

DEVELOPED
2016

WEIGHT
Up to 75 kg (165 lb)

HOW IT WORKS

Eelume is a flexible robot made of many joints and thrusters. It is powered via a connection to an operator station. Many remotely operated vehicles (ROVs) are too big to fit inside the limited space of underwater installations, but this robot's size and shape allow immediate and easy access. It can be lengthened and shortened depending on the requirements of each job, and can utilize a variety of tools and sensors for underwater inspection and repairs.

Different tools can be added to Eelume's main body.

> **“**Our vehicles are engineered to **live permanently under water**, where they can be mobilized 24/7 regardless of weather conditions.**”**
>
> **Eelume**

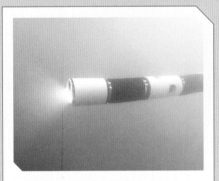

SWIM STAR

Trials have demonstrated Eelume's impressive performance at depths up to 150 m (492 ft) in challenging currents and stormy seas. By docking at designated stations on the seabed, it can stay underwater indefnitely, meaning bad weather on the surface poses no problem. The bot's fluid, smooth movement results in highly efficient cleaning and repairs, as well as detailed photographs and video footage.

The joint module extends or changes the bot's shape.

The front-facing HD camera can capture crystal-clear photographs and video footage.

The LED lights provide a clear view in even the murkiest ocean depths.

The longitudinal thruster module enables forward and backward movement.

The camera is attached to a swivel mechanism, and can rotate to cover every angle.

The tether module connects to an external power source to charge Eelume up.

GOING GREEN

Eelume provides an ecologically sound solution to underwater site management. In this line of work, surface vehicles must usually be deployed, but this aquatic bot can move out immediately from its permanent home on the seabed. Cameras along its body give the operator a clear view of ongoing inspections and repairs. As a result, safety comes first, costs are cut, and there is less impact on the environment.

The bot can attach itself to the site with one end, and work with the other end.

The lateral thruster module allows sideways hovering movement.

The slimline design ensures accurate manoeuvring in choppy currents.

WORK ROBOT

EELUME

Developed for underwater use, this self-propelled bot has a serpent-like agility and the streamlined swimming skills of an eel. Its body is made of modules that can be swapped and adapted to the task at hand. As oil and gas industries look for new ways to manage their off-shore installations, Eelume is at the forefront of the field of inspection, maintenance, and repair. Equipped with cameras, sensors, and a range of tools, this aquatic shape-shifter can be straight as a torpedo for long-distance travel, but agile and versatile enough to explore the places no diver or vessel can reach.

UNDERWATER STATION

Eelume can connect to a permanent docking station on the ocean floor with room for multiple underwater robots. Eelume can swim out from this base to inspect oil rigs and pipelines without using surface vessels. Future designs might be able to withstand greater pressure and go deeper for further research and repair.

MANUFACTURER
Festo

ORIGIN
Germany

HEIGHT
1 m (3.3 ft)

BIOMIMETIC ROBOT
Bionic Kangaroo

Everyone's favourite Australian animal has taken a technological twist in the form of the BionicKangaroo. This big bouncer can jump like a real kangaroo, reaching 40 cm (16 in) high over a distance of 80 cm (32 in). The German manufacturers studied the kangaroo's unique motion for two years before perfecting this artificial adaptation. A series of motors, sensors, and energy-storing legs ensure the BionicKangaroo never tires. Future endurance technology for robots and cars could be based on this marsupial model.

The foam body shell is strengthened with carbon to keep the robot lightweight.

The front legs are pulled forwards to increase the jumping distance during a hop.

The tail is a third point of contact with the ground to provide extra stability when standing.

SIDE VIEW

HOW IT WORKS

A kangaroo stores and releases energy for jumping via its version of the Achilles tendon (the tissue that connects the calf muscles to the heel). The robotic version uses a complex combination of pneumatic and electrical technology, together with an elastic spring made of rubber, to recreate this behaviour. A central control computer analyses data from the robot's sensors to determine how to position it for take-off and landing.

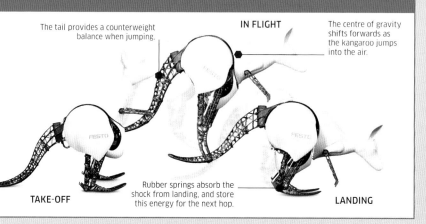

The tail provides a counterweight balance when jumping.

IN FLIGHT

The centre of gravity shifts forwards as the kangaroo jumps into the air.

TAKE-OFF

Rubber springs absorb the shock from landing, and store this energy for the next hop.

LANDING

The motor-controlled tail positions itself to provide stability and balance when standing, jumping, and landing.

An elastic rubber spring at the back of the foot emulates a kangaroo's Achilles tendon.

Cylinders of compressed air attached to each lower leg power the hop.

Long back legs contain sensors that gather data from the robot's environment.

ACTING ON DATA

A robot's CPU constantly receives feedback and information from the robot's sensors. Intelligent robots use this data to make all kinds of decisions. A roving robot's response to the information it has gathered can be varied – from imaging the environment, or using tools to examine and take samples, to giving up on that location altogether and navigating its way to another place. The data it receives may indicate that the robot is facing a dangerous situation. In this case, it may sound an alarm, send signals to its human controllers, or look to protect itself by making a hasty retreat.

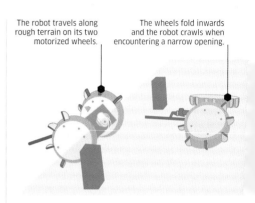

The robot travels along rough terrain on its two motorized wheels.

The wheels fold inwards and the robot crawls when encountering a narrow opening.

Shape-shifting

A small number of robots have a very dramatic response to the data they collect – they change shape. These robots alter their form for a variety of potential reasons. It might help them complete their task, such as a tall mobile robot altering shape to form a low, stable solid base so that it can lift and move heavy objects. On other occasions, a change of shape might help the robot navigate through different terrain – for example, if a land-robot changes itself to be able to move on water.

Different environments

Some robots act on the data they gather by physically interacting with their surroundings. They might find things, such as an underwater salvage robot finding and recovering shipwreck treasures. Others take samples of the water, soil, or air around them for transport back to a laboratory for scientific analysis.

Water sampling

The LRI Wave Glider robot lacks the ability to move. It drifts on the ocean waves as its probes gather and test the water for temperature, oxygen levels, and salt and pollution levels.

The robot is powered by solar panels.

Rero

This toy robot features modular parts that can be combined and arranged in a variety of ways, including a spider bot (above) and humanoid (below). Future robots may adopt a similar modular construction, but be able to reconfigure themselves to alter their form and function.

The robot can also take plant samples for further analysis.

Soil sampling

Soil-sampling robots burrow into the soil and take a cylindrical core sample. This can be sent to a science laboratory to test how acidic the soil is (its pH level) and the levels of nutrients vital for plant growth, such as potassium, it contains.

The gathered air sample is pumped into this bag.

Air sampling

Drones can be used to monitor air quality or monitor atmospheric pollution from chemical plants and power stations. Some drones can perform sample-testing on board the robot, checking for the concentration of potentially harmful pollutants.

Obstacle | The wheels can unfold when the space ahead of the robot opens up.

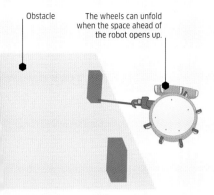

PUFFER

Designed by NASA, the PUFFER (short for Pop-Up Flat Folding Explorer Robot) prototype is designed to head into lava tubes, narrow caves, and rocky crevices, exploring as it goes. It can alter its shape to squeeze under particularly tight ledges and through low gaps.

Soft robots

A soft robot with a flexible X-shaped body made of silicone rubber can survive squashing and changes of shape. Soft robots like this one are modelled on animals that can change body shape to squeeze through small gaps, such as octopus and squid.

ATRON

This robot consists of independently-powered spheres that can latch onto one another to form a variety of robots, including a legged walker, a long snakebot, and a wheeled rover.

ROVER

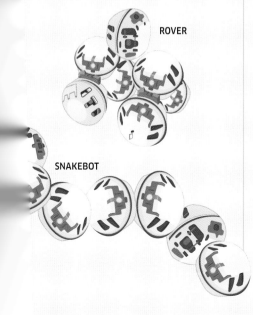

SNAKEBOT

Asking for help

If a robot cannot manoeuvre around danger itself, it may be able to decide to call for help. This might involve alerting its human controllers to end its mission and retrieve the bot, or possibly to summon other robots for assistance. Collaborative robotics is a growing field and may one day yield multi-robot teams that mostly work individually but can band together when a task requires a group effort. A two-robot system, for instance, can involve an aerial or underwater robot collecting and delivering a land robot to a destination it could not get to alone.

Helping push

Individual robot workers such as these could primarily work on their own, but come together to help each other with tasks. If one struggled to travel up a steep incline, for example, it might summon help from the others to use their combined power to push it up the slope.

The robots connect using electromagnet links that can be switched on or off.

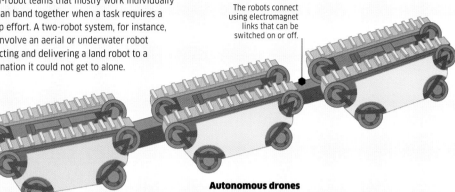

Autonomous drones

A solar panel array in a desert can harvest a lot of energy from the sun, but only if desert dust does not cloud the panels. An autonomous drone could pick up and ferry cleaning robots to the panels, and collect them when the panel is cleaned.

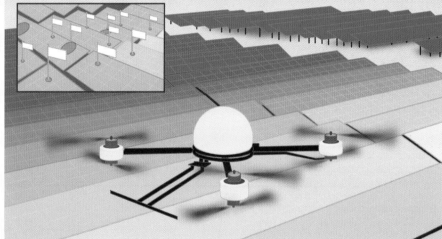

1 The drone hovers above solar panels and identifies those parts most covered in sand and dust.

2 The drone collects and flies the cleaning robot to the solar panels.

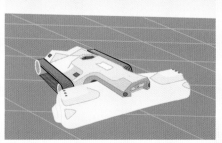

3 The cleaning robot travels across the panel, wiping it clean of dust.

MANUFACTURER
Harvard University

ORIGIN
USA

DEVELOPED
2013

Each wing can be controlled separately.

This thin plastic hinge embedded in the RoboBee's body acts as one of its wing joints.

The ceramic actuators are attached to the side of the bot's carbon fibre body.

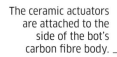

WINGS

The robot's wings are made from a thin film supported by a very slender framework made of carbon fibre strands. Earlier versions of the RoboBee's wing featured a lattice pattern frame (right).

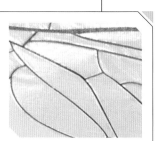

HOW THEY WORK

Tiny ceramic actuators, nicknamed "flight muscles", provide the robot's propulsion. These work by changing their length when an electric current is applied. The actuators' movement is converted into rapid flapping (around 120 beats per second) controlled by joints found on the robot's shoulder. The angle of the wings and their flapping pattern can be altered so that the robot can change its direction in all three dimensions – pitch, roll, and yaw.

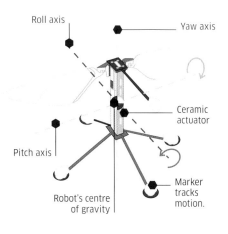

Roll axis

Yaw axis

Ceramic actuator

Pitch axis

Marker tracks motion.

Robot's centre of gravity

HEIGHT
2 cm (0.75 in)

WEIGHT
0.175 g (0.006 oz)

POWER
Integrated
power source

HYBRID BOT

A new RoboBee, developed in 2017, can fly, swim, and dive in and out of water. The bot is fitted with four boxes on its arms, known as outriggers, which help it to float on water. A chemical reaction helps it propel out of the water.

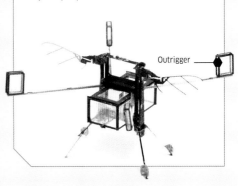

Outrigger

A RoboBee's wingspan is 3 cm (1.2 in).

> **❝It is a centimetre-scale, biologically inspired flapping wing aerial vehicle.❞**
>
> *Elizabeth Farrell Helbling,*
> Research Assistant, **Harvard University**

The markers on the ends of the bot's legs can be spotted by motion capture cameras to track its movement as it flies.

SWARM ROBOT

RoboBees

Great things do come in very small packages. The RoboBees are tiny flying robots developed by engineers at Harvard University, USA. Assembled by hand under a microscope, RoboBees are fabricated from single sheets of carbon fibre, which are assembled and glued. RoboBees made their first controlled flight in 2013. They can take off and make short flights, changing direction easily and even hovering in mid-air. Each RoboBee weighs as little as 0.08 g (0.003 oz) – it would take a dozen of these miniscule mini-bots to equal the weight of a jelly bean.

SMALLEST DRONE

At such small scales, it wasn't possible to install an on-board power source on the bot, such as a rechargeable battery, so the designers provided power supply via a hair-thin electrical tether that trails below the robot (right). Further advances have seen RoboBees fitted with an antenna to measure wind strength and a simple light sensor to detect the Sun so the robot knows which direction is upwards.

A US penny (1 cent coin) is 30 times heavier than a RoboBee.

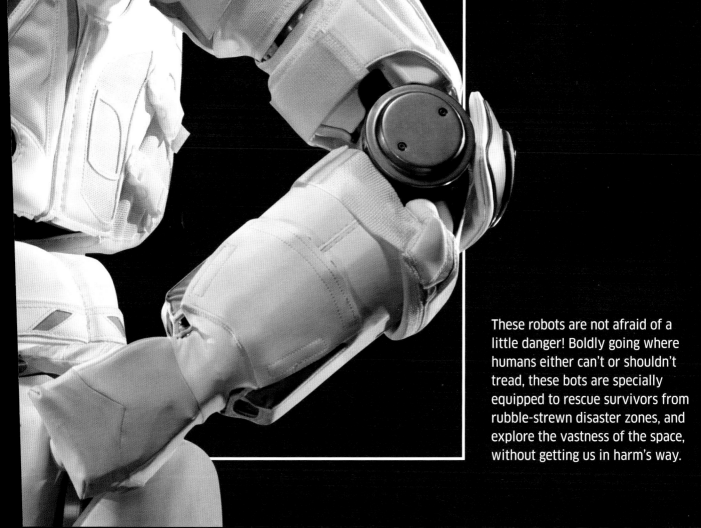

HERO
BOTS

These robots are not afraid of a
little danger! Boldly going where
humans either can't or shouldn't
tread, these bots are specially
equipped to rescue survivors from
rubble-strewn disaster zones, and
explore the vastness of the space,
without getting us in harm's way.

MANUFACTURER
NASA

ORIGIN
USA

SCHEDULED
2020

HEIGHT
2.1 m (7 ft)

WEIGHT
1,050 kg (2,315 lb)

HOW IT WORKS

Mars 2020 is a rolling science lab, packed with scientific instruments and experiments as well as 23 cameras to document and further understand the geology of Mars, and to find out if life existed there in the past. One of the instruments – MOXIE – seeks to turn samples of Mars's thin atmosphere (containing 95 per cent carbon dioxide) into oxygen – a gas crucial to chances of a future human-supporting Mars base.

The SuperCam will fire a laser to vaporize small areas of rock for analysing their composition.

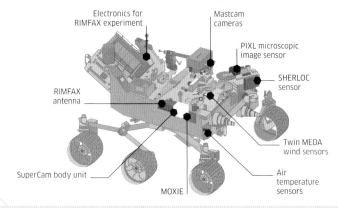

Electronics for RIMFAX experiment

Mastcam cameras

PIXL microscopic image sensor

SHERLOC sensor

RIMFAX antenna

Twin MEDA wind sensors

SuperCam body unit

Air temperature sensors

MOXIE

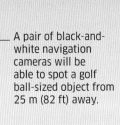

A pair of black-and-white navigation cameras will be able to spot a golf ball-sized object from 25 m (82 ft) away.

The front cameras will help detect obstacles and targets ahead.

The 52.5-cm- (20.7-in-) wide aluminium wheels will allow the rover to ride over knee-high rocks.

POWER
Generator using
radioactive isotope

SPACE ROBOT

MARS 2020

Hefty and rugged, the latest in a long line of NASA rovers will reach Mars after a nine-month journey through space following its expected launch in 2020. It will be working on its own on the rocky and sandy planet about 225 million km (140 million miles) away from Earth – the same distance as 586 trips from Earth to the Moon. It therefore needs to be both tough and smart, to be able to navigate itself, and to tackle steep slopes. Multiple tools on the end of its 2.1-m- (7-ft-) long robotic arm can drill holes in rock, extract samples, take microscopic images, and analyse the make up of Martian rocks and soil.

PRESERVING SAMPLES

One of the rover's key tasks will be to drill down to collect core samples of rock 5 cm (2 in) below the surface of Mars. It will store these samples in individual, sealed tubes inside its body until mission control back on Earth commands the rover to create a cache (store) of tubes on the planet's surface. The rover will note the precise location of the cache for potential recovery by future missions.

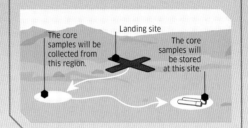

The core samples will be collected from this region.

Landing site

The core samples will be stored at this site.

BUILDING THE ROVER

Construction of the car-sized robot involves thousands of specialist technicians working on different parts of its structure, electronics, and sensors. The rover's 3-m-(10-ft-) long body contains heaters to protect its sensitive electronics from Mars's cripplingly cold environment.

"This mission will further our search for life in the Universe."

John Grunsfeld, Astronaut and Associate Administrator, **NASA**

The SHERLOC instrument will scan the surface with a laser to detect organic chemicals from possible living things.

Remote piloting

Large numbers of robots working in disaster zones and other hazardous environments are remote-controlled. A human operator can be in constant command of the robot, guiding its movement using a joystick, touchpad, or some other computer input device. The instructions can be sent along cables when the robot is operating close by. Most systems, though, transmit commands wirelessly using radio signals, allowing the operator to stay safely away from danger.

FINDING A WAY

Mobile robots need to travel to specific places to perform their work. The paths some bots take are controlled by a human, but others are capable of going it alone and finding their own way. Finding a stable path to a destination can be especially difficult for robots working in unknown terrain, or unsafe environments, such as a rubble-strewn disaster zone. In these scenarios, the robot may have to both detect and find a way around obstacles in its path.

1 Deployment
Rugged yet weighing just 5 kg (11 lb), the Dragon Runner robot can be hurled round corners or thrown through building windows to investigate a suspicious device such as a bomb or booby trap.

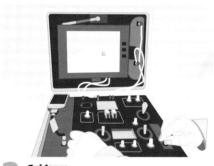

2 Guidance
Using wireless communication links, human operators remotely control the robot's movement from a safe distance using a laptop computer or handheld controller. The robot's camera feed is used by the operator to plot its route.

3 Action
The operator can also command the robot to perform a variety of actions, such as opening doors, cutting cables, or even defusing a bomb.

Human and machine

Some robots are partly smart. They may be mostly remote controlled by humans but do have some autonomy and make their own decisions during certain parts of their tasks. Some roving exploration robots, for instance, are given their destination by human operators but choose themselves how to plot a path and make their way to their target. In 2017, one partly smart underwater robot called

Mini Manbo embarked on a hazardous mission through the flooded remains of the damaged Fukushima nuclear power plant in Japan. It was guided by humans, but could override their control if its sensors detected it getting too close to a highly radioactive "hot spot". The robot successfully tracked down and discovered the nuclear plant's missing uranium fuel, an achievement that had eluded other searches for six years.

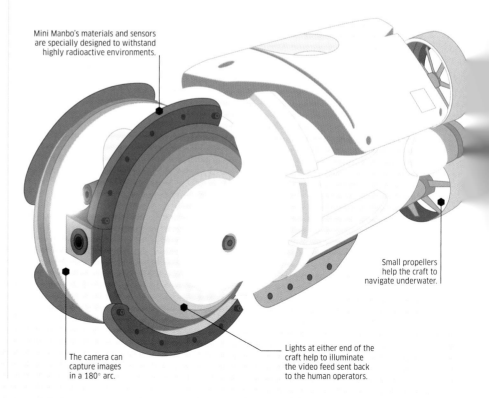

Mini Manbo's materials and sensors are specially designed to withstand highly radioactive environments.

The camera can capture images in a 180° arc.

Small propellers help the craft to navigate underwater.

Lights at either end of the craft help to illuminate the video feed sent back to the human operators.

Detecting obstacles

To travel freely, a robot needs to know what obstacles lie in its path, and precisely where they are located. The most simple of obstacle detection sensors are contact sensors, which register a signal when they physically touch another object. These come in many forms, from antennae or whisker-like feelers to switches on the bumpers of automated guided vehicles. Other sensors send out streams of light or sound to detect obstacles before the robot gets too close.

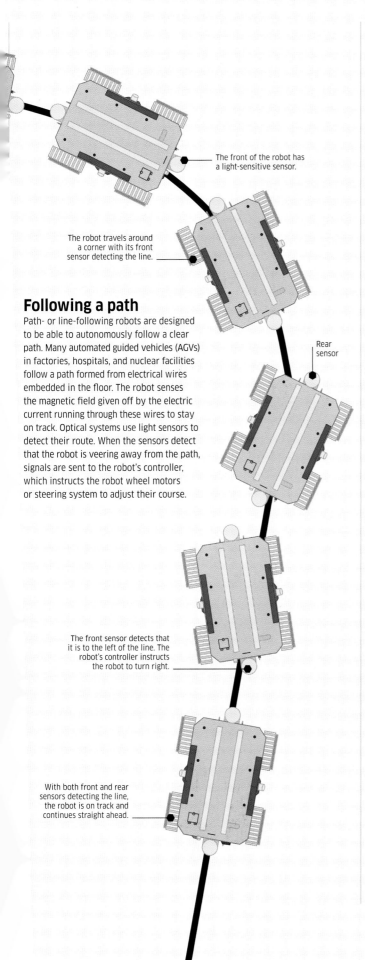

The front of the robot has a light-sensitive sensor.

The robot travels around a corner with its front sensor detecting the line.

Following a path

Path- or line-following robots are designed to be able to autonomously follow a clear path. Many automated guided vehicles (AGVs) in factories, hospitals, and nuclear facilities follow a path formed from electrical wires embedded in the floor. The robot senses the magnetic field given off by the electric current running through these wires to stay on track. Optical systems use light sensors to detect their route. When the sensors detect that the robot is veering away from the path, signals are sent to the robot's controller, which instructs the robot wheel motors or steering system to adjust their course.

Rear sensor

The front sensor detects that it is to the left of the line. The robot's controller instructs the robot to turn right.

With both front and rear sensors detecting the line, the robot is on track and continues straight ahead.

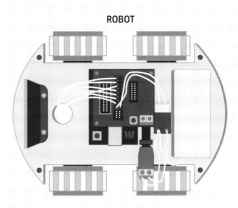

OBSTACLE

ROBOT

Infrared

Infrared distance sensors work by sending out beams of infrared light, invisible to the human eye. The light reflects off any surfaces it strikes, and is gathered in by one or more infrared receivers. The length of time this takes, and the angle at which the light returns, help the robot to calculate how far away and where the obstacle is.

Avoiding a fall

Cliff sensors are fitted to the underside or edge of some mobile robots, particularly robotic vacuum cleaners. The sensor faces downwards and bounces sound or light off surfaces. If the signal is not returned immediately, it means the robot is close to a ledge, which causes it to change direction.

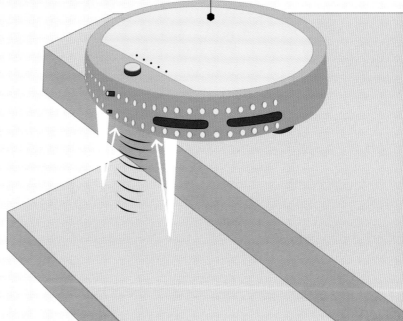

Vacuum cleaning robot approaches top of stairs. Its cliff sensor will alert it to reverse its direction to stop itself from falling.

MANUFACTURER
The Ripper
Group International

ORIGIN
Australia

RELEASED
2016

WEIGHT
15 kg (33 lb)

HOW DRONES WORK

Unmanned aerial vehicles (UAVs), commonly known as drones, are perfect for rescue missions. Operators can control the drone remotely from another location. The drone uses battery power to operate the rotor motors and turn the propellers for flight. Drones are used all over the world, especially where human-flown aircraft would be too big or dangerous. They can assist in war zones and disaster situations, map and inspect territory, or can be flown just for fun.

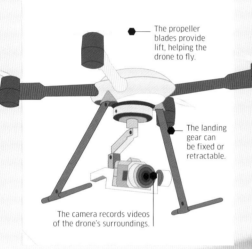

The propeller blades provide lift, helping the drone to fly.

The landing gear can be fixed or retractable.

The camera records videos of the drone's surroundings.

The drone's lightweight propellers allow it to fly smoothly, keeping it stable in flight.

RESCUE

PILOTED ROBOT

LITTLE RIPPER LIFESAVER

Unpredictable currents and hungry sharks can make surfing and swimming dangerous activities. Helping to keep people safer on Australian beaches is the Little Ripper Lifesaver. This is a high-tech drone that can spot sharks, sound alarms, look for missing people, drop emergency supplies, and bring flotation pods. The Little Ripper Lifesaver moves fast and travels far – reaching a top speed of 64 km/h (40 mph) and flying as far as 1.5 km (0.9 miles) out to sea. It works well in extreme weather and challenging locations, putting it at the forefront of modern search and rescue technology. In 2018, the Little Ripper Lifesaver saved two swimmers caught out in turbulent waters off the coast of New South Wales, Australia, by dropping an inflatable pod to carry them ashore.

SHARK SPOTTING

The Little Ripper Lifesaver features SharkSpotter technology, which can identify and track sharks in the local area, before hovering over swimmers or surfers to warn them of the danger using its loudspeaker. It can also identify other objects in water, including boats, whales, rays, and dolphins. Live video taken by the drone can be transmitted in real time to lifeguards in beach towers and clubs.

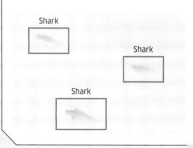

Shark

Shark

Shark

POWER
Battery

FEATURES
Camera, speaker system,
artificial intelligence,
and remote control

The cameras are used to
explore, investigate, and
keep watch over areas
of sea determined by
the remote operator.

If required, a flotation
device or rescue pack
can be dropped from the
drone by the operator.

RIPPER RESCUE

In case of an emergency, the Little Ripper Lifesaver drops a flotation device, which
inflates upon impact with the water. This device can hold up to four adults for
24 hours in the water. The drone uses an on-board loudspeaker system to explain
how to use the device, and to confirm that an emergency rescue is on the way.

Little Ripper Lifesaver spots
people in distress

Drone drops flotation device that
inflates in water

Rescued people use float to
help them swim ashore

| Hankook Mirae Technology | South Korea | 4.2 m (13.8 ft) | 1.5 tonnes |

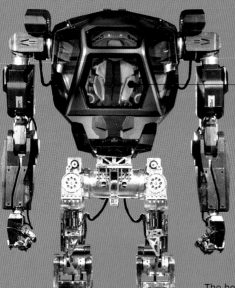

The protective glass cockpit keeps the pilot safe while working in hazardous environments.

The bot can walk forwards and backwards, tethered to a pair of steel power cables that help keep its balance.

FRONT VIEW

GET IN

Method-2 follows its pilot's commands. Sitting inside a cockpit sealed to give protection from environmental hazards, the pilot makes movements via levers and the bot copies them – if the pilot raises an arm, so does the bot. Since it is a little wobbly on its feet, the cockpit has cushioning to protect the pilot from the impact of shaky movement.

Movements are controlled by two mechanical levers.

> **"Our robot ... is built to work in extreme hazardous areas where humans cannot go"**
> *Yang Jin-Ho, Chairman, Hankook Mirae Technology*

The arms and torso are made of an aluminium alloy and carbon fibre.

FIERCE GRIP

More than 40 computer-controlled motors housed in Method-2's torso help transmit the pilot's movements to the arms, hands, and fingers, giving the pilot an incredible level of control and accuracy over the robot's movements.

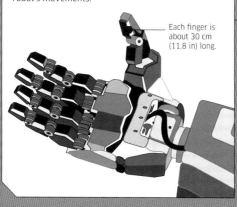

Each finger is about 30 cm (11.8 in) long.

The bot's lower body is completely made of aluminium alloy.

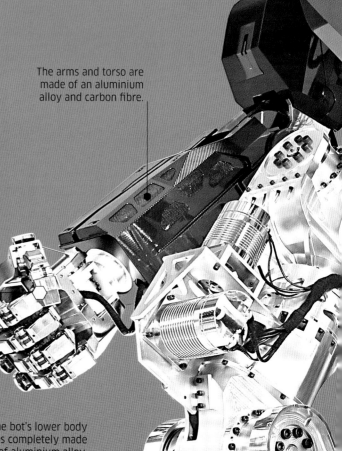

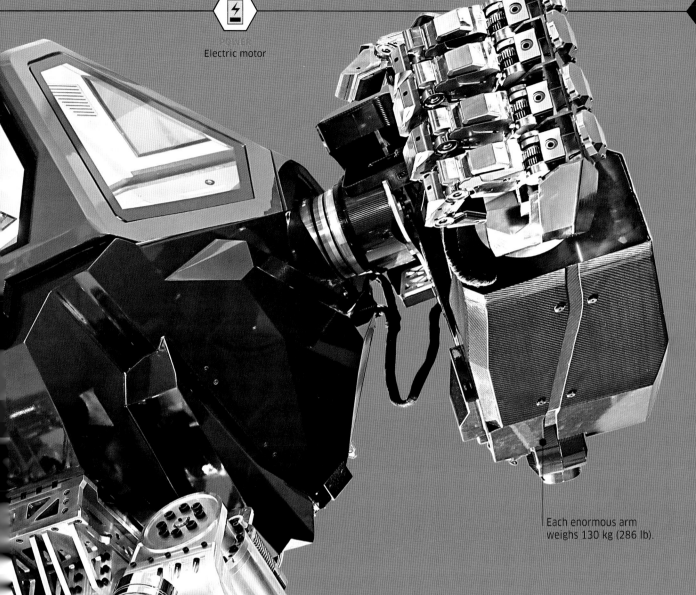

POWER
Electric motor

Each enormous arm weighs 130 kg (286 lb).

PILOTED ROBOT

METHOD-2

With its enormous size and ground-shaking weight, Method-2 has stomped into the tech world as the first bipedal robot to be piloted by a human inside. This hulking bot was created to work in very dangerous places, such as ruins left behind by nuclear explosions, where humans cannot go without protection. Safe inside the cockpit, its human controller moves the robot through a number of tasks. A team of 45 engineers have built and tested each of the bot's cables, motors, nuts, and bolts. Method-2's movie-star looks are no coincidence, as its designer also works on robot concepts for big-budget cinema blockbusters and video games.

◄ Cylinder-shaped Luigi is controlled by smartphone, and researchers at street level use GPS devices to track it.

A pack of batteries powers the sewage bot.

The pump sucks up samples in the same way as a vacuum cleaner sucks up dirt.

The sample is pushed through a filter to prevent water, toilet paper, and other waste from entering.

Sensors keep the robot hovering 40 cm (16 in) above its target.

SEWER PATROL

The first automated sewage-searching robot, **Luigi** is happy to get down and dirty collecting waste beneath the streets of some American cities. The samples may be stinky, but they provide scientists with information about bacteria, viruses, and diseases living inside the human body. The findings build up a clear view of a city's health and can predict future patterns of disease. Similar smart sewage systems are set to spread around the world.

▲ Lowered manually into sewage drains, Luigi surveys for about an hour, collecting samples from the sewage that passes by.

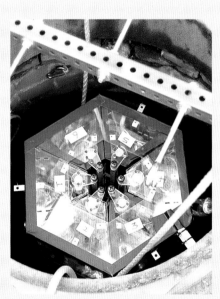

▲ Luigi's predecessor was the robot Mario, which was equipped with sewage-sucking syringes. However, its design was flawed, so the Luigi robot was developed as an improvement.

▲ This drone can fly for 10 km (6 miles) at speeds of 40 km/h (25 mph) for four hours.

SURVEILLANCE DRONE

The **Lockheed Martin Indago** is used in all kinds of operations – from search and rescue to disaster relief. Before a mission, a remote operator first chooses a suitable payload or surveillance for the task. The lightweight, portable quad-copter is then unfolded in 60 seconds and is airborne in just over two minutes whatever the weather. A wireless hand controller with a touchscreen keeps track of its movements in the skies, while video footage is live-streamed back to the screen.

ASSISTING DOCTORS

Robots and AI are also helping people, such as soldiers, who return from pressurized situations. The virtual human **Ellie** was created to help people suffering from stress disorders to be able to talk about their feelings, after studies found that people could be more open with someone anonymous. This AI robot operates automatically, using computer algorithms to determine its speech, gestures, and movements. Ellie has already interacted with 600 patients for training purposes.

SimSensei

MultiSense

▲ Ellie's sophisticated AI can read and respond to human conversation in real time.

DANGER ZONES

Robots have emerged as modern-day heroes by doing some of the world's most challenging work. When the going gets tough, tough robot workers get going. This is not technology taking over, but robots braving danger zones that humans would rather not enter. From wading through waste to clearing out chemicals, these robots make themselves at home in the most difficult, dirty, and dangerous places, making sure that humans do not risk their health or their lives for these hazardous jobs.

SAFETY INSPECTOR

The portable **PackBot** is used on dangerous missions, including chemical detection, building clearance, and bomb disposal. Two gaming-style hand controllers are used to remotely operate the robot. It features a range of sensors, cameras, and payloads to carry out safety inspections. At least 2,000 PackBots have been deployed in Iraq and Afghanistan, and 5,000 more are used by defence teams around the world.

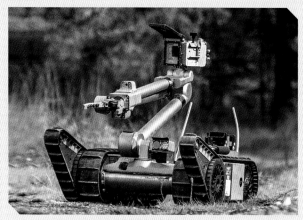

▲ Moving at speeds of 9 km/h (5.5 mph), PackBot can navigate any surroundings, including grass, snow, rock, rubble, and water.

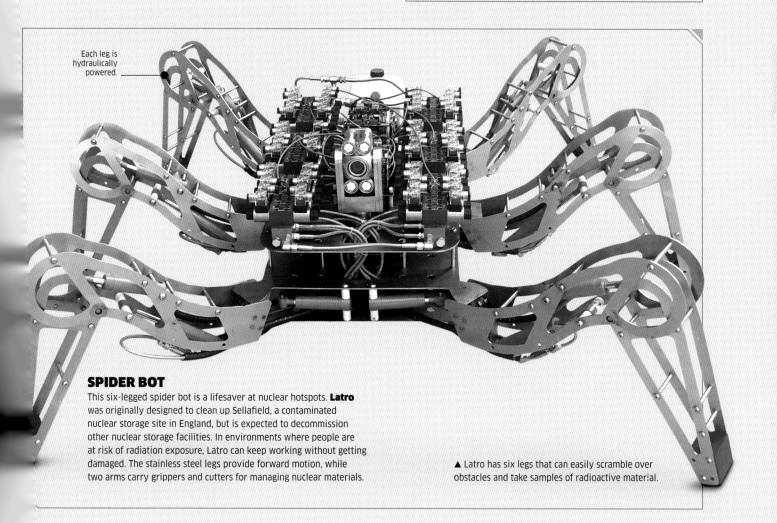

Each leg is hydraulically powered.

SPIDER BOT

This six-legged spider bot is a lifesaver at nuclear hotspots. **Latro** was originally designed to clean up Sellafield, a contaminated nuclear storage site in England, but is expected to decommission other nuclear storage facilities. In environments where people are at risk of radiation exposure, Latro can keep working without getting damaged. The stainless steel legs provide forward motion, while two arms carry grippers and cutters for managing nuclear materials.

▲ Latro has six legs that can easily scramble over obstacles and take samples of radioactive material.

MANUFACTURER	ORIGIN	DEVELOPED	WEIGHT
Sarcos	USA	2015	7.2 kg (16 lb)

WORK ROBOT

GUARDIAN™ S

The Guardian™ S snakebot can stealthily slither into the world's most dangerous situations, providing two-way voice, video, and data communication with a human operator back at base. Packed with sensors and cameras, this portable powerhouse carries out surveillance and inspection in the most hazardous locations and disaster areas. The lifesaving technology can check for poisonous gas, radiation, and harmful chemicals without posing any risk to human life. Confined spaces and rough terrain are no problem for Guardian™ S, which has magnetized tracks for skilful sliding in any direction.

VERTICAL LIMIT

On horizontal surfaces, the snakebot can carry loads of up to 4.5 kg (10 lb), while on the steepest walls, the bot's magnetized body can slither up at dramatic angles. It stays balanced while navigating through snow, rubble, mud, or water. Enclosed spaces, such as narrow pipes and storage tanks, are ideal spaces to test this compact technology. Even when structures have collapsed or become unstable, Guardian™ S can enter and explore in detail without endangering the lives of human helpers.

The sensors along the bot's body provide real-time data, such as temperature and humidity.

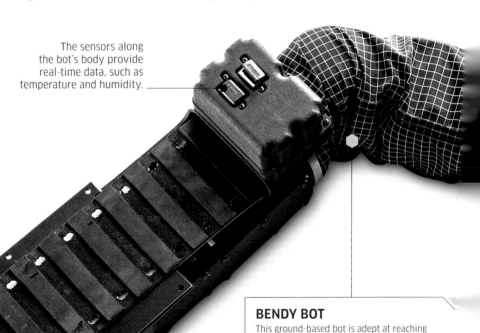

The forward and rear tracks enhance the bot's mobility.

Its magnetized body allows the robot to climb up walls and stairs.

BENDY BOT

This ground-based bot is adept at reaching places that are inaccessible to humans. Thanks to the mobile treads on either end, Guardian™ S can easily glide up stairs. Its bendy body makes light work of sharp turns and is rugged enough to keep rolling on all kinds of terrain.

EXTREME PLACES

Guardian™ S is at home in the most dangerous and deadly terrain. It can assist in many operations, including bomb disposal, rescue and recovery, fire prevention, and surveillance tasks. First on the scene, this snake-like robot can take readings and collate data before professionals positioned at a safe distance away are given the all clear to start work. Guardian™ S is water-tight and can be decontaminated after exposure to hazardous materials.

The LED light illuminates dark places.

The bot's flat design allows entry into tight openings measuring just 18 cm (7 in).

HOW IT WORKS

Guardian™ S is carried by hand to the inspection site or disaster area. The operator turns the robot on, and wirelessly connects it to a special operating pendant that is fitted with joysticks similar to those on a games console. The operator can then steer the bot from afar, and track its movements on a screen.

This snakebot can move in all directions, feeding data and footage back to the operator, as well as marking the coordinates of trouble spots. Analysts in different locations can study and share the information before agreeing on a plan of action. Guardian™ S can cover a distance of 4.8 km (3 miles) on one charge.

Guardian™ S is lowered or placed by hand into the inspection area, where it can snake sideways into tight spaces.

It can perform a 360° roll if required, or to right itself if it is flipped over.

The bendy middle section gives the robot a great degree of flexibility to operate in awkward areas.

MANUFACTURER
Carnegie Mellon
University

ORIGIN
USA

DEVELOPED
2013

PILOTED ROBOT
CHIMP

There is no monkey business with Chimp (Carnegie Mellon University Highly Intelligent Mobile Platform). This rescue robot could be crucial in an emergency, bringing vital assistance in the most challenging situations. Robot humanoids can struggle to balance on two legs, but Chimp overcomes this with strong, stabilizing, motorized treads on all four limbs to move, turn, and climb with ease. Chimp has opposable thumbs, which help it to grasp effectively in restricted spaces. Chimp brings the best in rescue robotics by combining strength and stability with dexterity and capability.

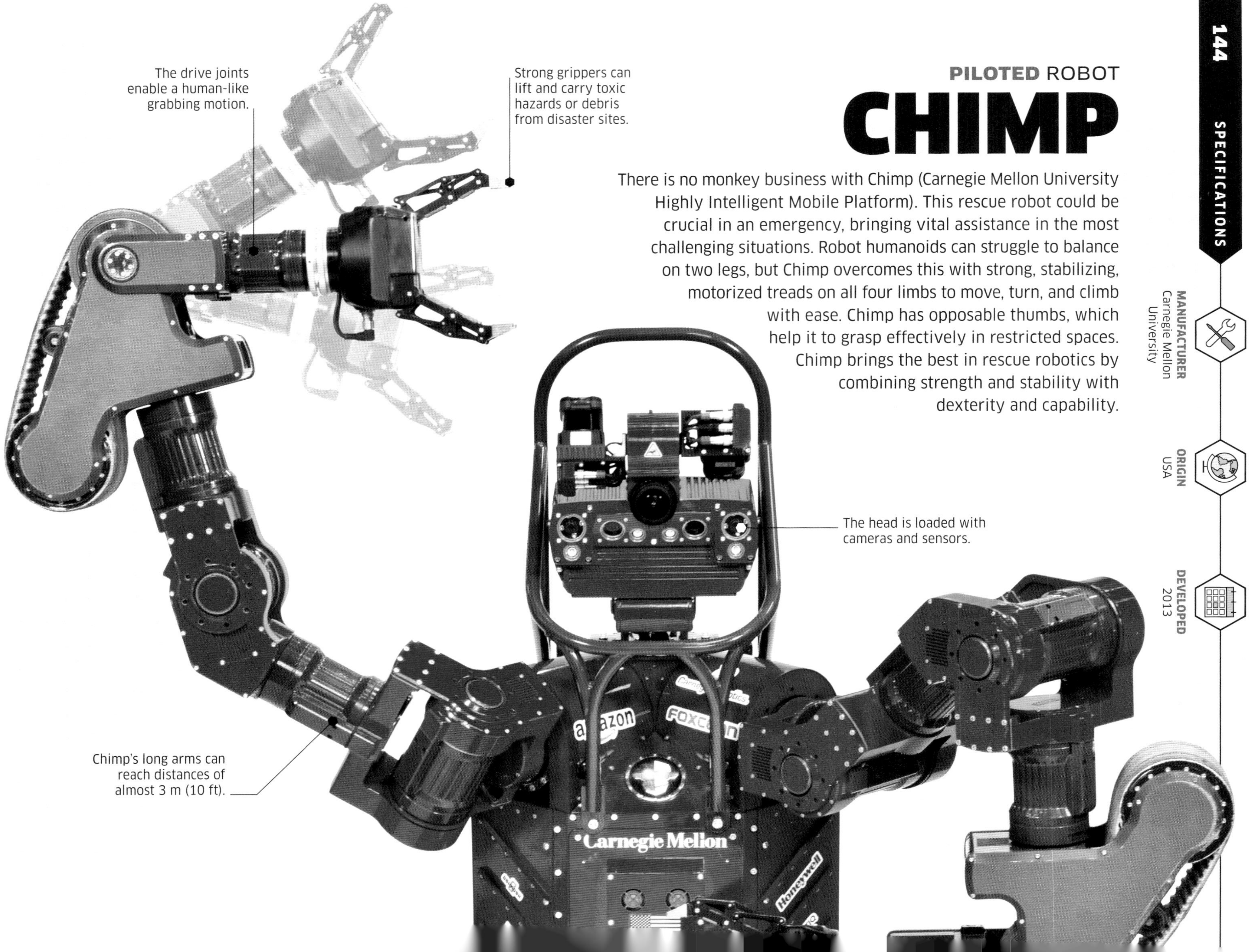

The head is loaded with cameras and sensors.

Strong grippers can lift and carry toxic hazards or debris from disaster sites.

The drive joints enable a human-like grabbing motion.

Chimp's long arms can reach distances of almost 3 m (10 ft).

HEIGHT
1.4 m (4.5 ft)

WEIGHT
200 kg (441 lb)

POWER
External tethered
power supply

FEATURES
Lasers, sensors,
cameras, and motors

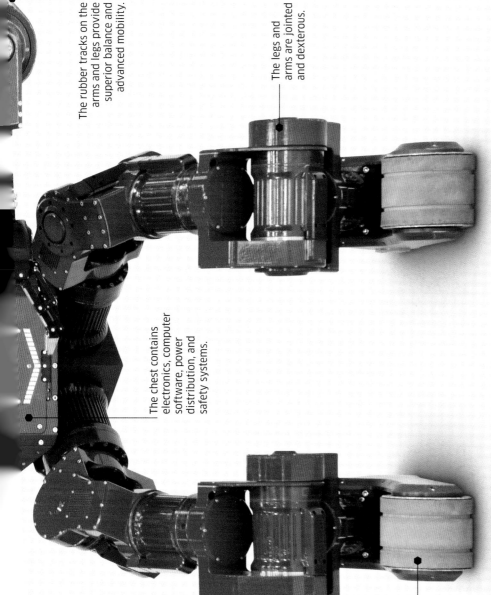

The rubber tracks on the arms and legs provide superior balance and advanced mobility.

The legs and arms are jointed and dexterous.

The chest contains electronics, computer software, power distribution, and safety systems.

The rollers on the feet allow the bot to move smoothly.

" Chimp is never at **risk of falling** over and is never actively balancing, because it doesn't have to. **"**

Clark Haynes, **Carnegie Mellon University**

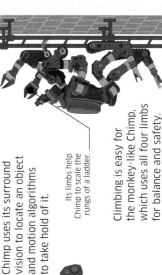

Chimp uses its surround vision to locate an object and motion algorithms to take hold of it.

Its limbs help Chimp to scale the rungs of a ladder.

Climbing is easy for the monkey-like Chimp, which uses all four limbs for balance and safety.

The flexible grippers hold and turn a wheel.

The tracks on Chimp's limbs provide stability and mobility for moving on two feet.

The balanced stance is exceptional for a humanoid robot.

HOW IT WORKS

Chimp has six cameras and LiDAR (light radar) sensors inside its head, which give the remote human operator a 3D view of the bot's immediate surroundings. The operator manually controls Chimp's movements and actions, but the robot can also be programmed to work autonomously.

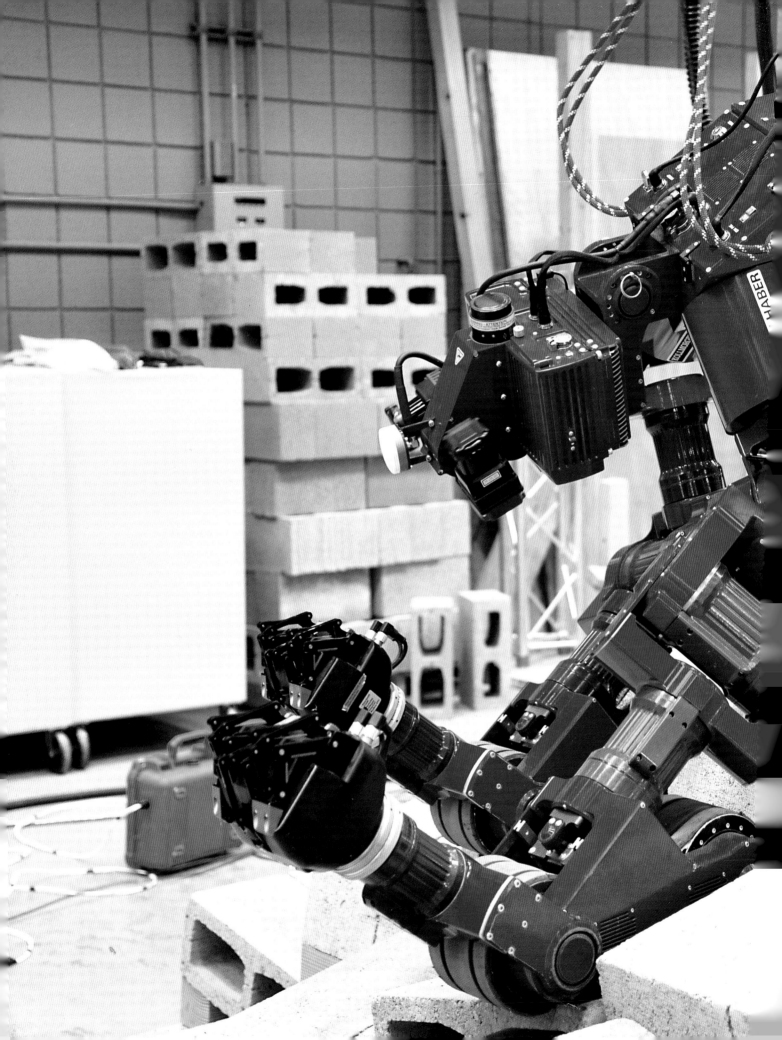

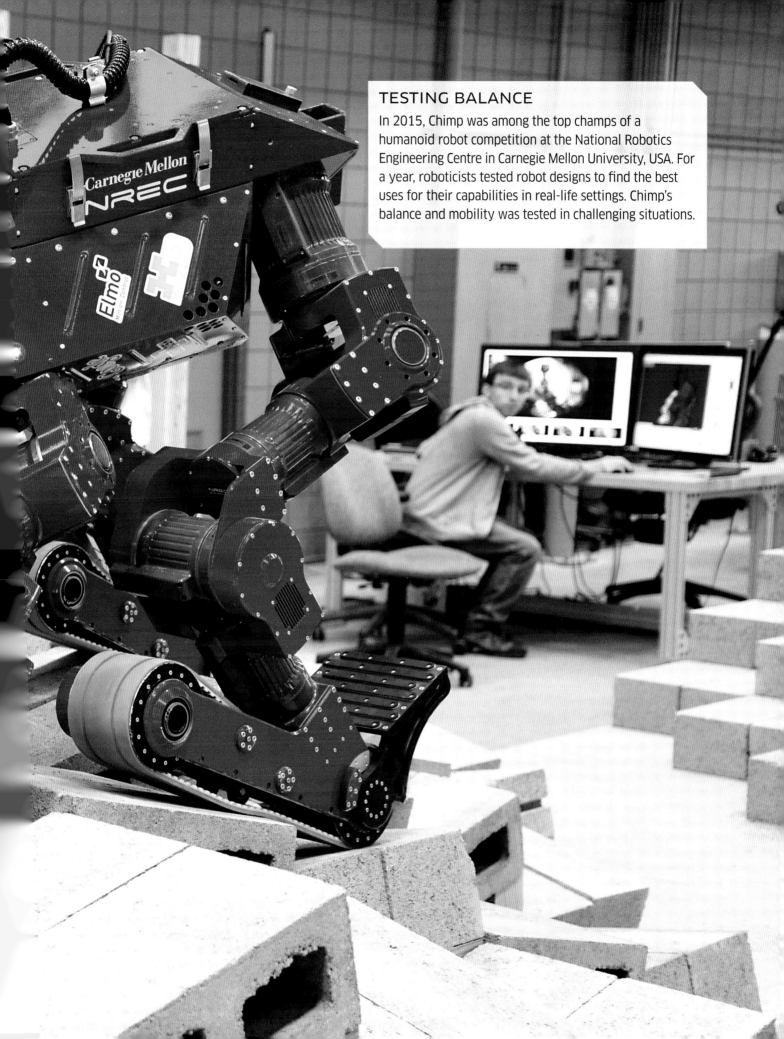

TESTING BALANCE

In 2015, Chimp was among the top champs of a humanoid robot competition at the National Robotics Engineering Centre in Carnegie Mellon University, USA. For a year, roboticists tested robot designs to find the best uses for their capabilities in real-life settings. Chimp's balance and mobility was tested in challenging situations.

FIGURING TERRAIN

Humans are pretty good at figuring out where they are – a skill known as localization. They may recognize objects and places around them, and sometimes use sensory cues, such as "hearing traffic means a road is nearby". Robots, in contrast, do not come with an inbuilt sense of where they are. They must be equipped with sensors and sophisticated algorithms in their software that together work to localize the robot and allow it to plan its next move.

Global positioning system

A network of more than 30 satellites in orbit around Earth provide accurate localization information to robots and other devices equipped with a GPS receiver. The receiver measures the time taken for signals sent from the satellites to reach it and converts this into distance away. Knowing the precise distances from three satellites allows the receiver to use trilateration to calculate its exact position on Earth. When four or more GPS satellites are tracked, the receiver's position and its altitude can be figured out.

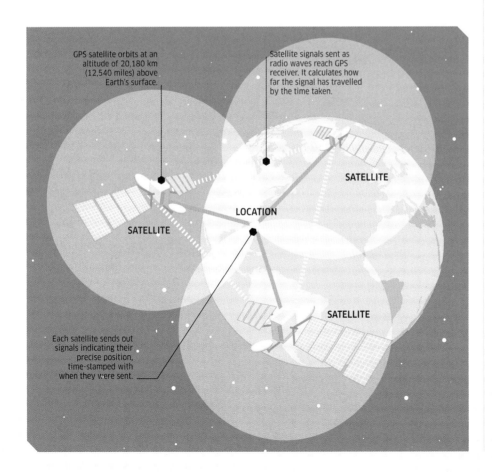

GPS satellite orbits at an altitude of 20,180 km (12,540 miles) above Earth's surface.

Satellite signals sent as radio waves reach GPS receiver. It calculates how far the signal has travelled by the time taken.

SATELLITE

SATELLITE

LOCATION

SATELLITE

Each satellite sends out signals indicating their precise position, time-stamped with when they were sent.

Making maps

Some robots, especially those working in space or in dangerous places on Earth, build up maps of their surroundings that they can understand and work with. Mars Exploration Rovers (MER) are given a target to head to on Mars by mission control on Earth, but are left to compute their best path to the destination. The robots achieve this task using their cameras and terrain-mapping software.

1 Imaging
The rover's stereo cameras take images of the landscape ahead. These are merged to give a simple depth map. The distances to a large number of individual points on the terrain – as many as 16,000 – are also calculated.

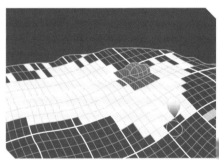

2 Terrain difficulty
The rover's software assesses the terrain, measuring the steepness of slopes and how rough or smooth they are. The areas are colour-coded for ease of travel across them, with the most difficult areas shown here in red.

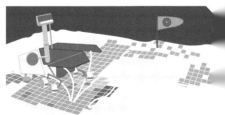

3 Route picked
The software calculates a number of different paths to its target. It compares them for speed and safety and picks the optimum path. As the rover travels on this route, the entire mapping process is repeated many times.

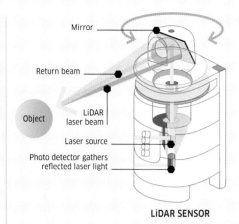

Mirror

Return beam

Object

LiDAR
laser beam

Laser source

Photo detector gathers
reflected laser light

LiDAR SENSOR

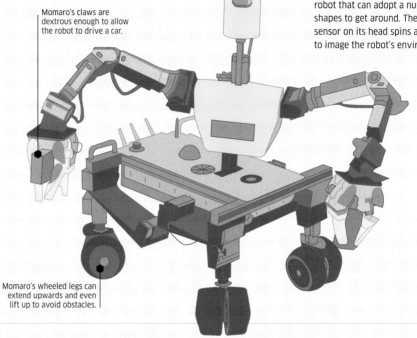

The images produced by LiDAR
can be coloured to make
elevation or distance clearer.

LiDAR
sensor

Momaro
Built by the University of Bonn,
Germany, Momaro is a flexible
robot that can adopt a number of
shapes to get around. The LiDAR
sensor on its head spins around
to image the robot's environment.

Momaro's claws are
dextrous enough to allow
the robot to drive a car.

Momaro's wheeled legs can
extend upwards and even
lift up to avoid obstacles.

LiDAR

A light-detection and ranging (LiDAR) sensor bounces
light energy off its surroundings to build up a map
of a robot's local environment. The light reflects
off objects and is re-gathered by photo detectors,
which calculate the distance to the object using
the time taken for it to return. First deployed on
aircraft to map the land below, LiDAR is now used
in driverless cars, UAVs, and other robots. Some
LiDAR systems send out 150,000 laser pulses
every second as they sweep round, to build a
very detailed depth map around the robot.

Sonar

An acronym for "sound navigation and ranging",
sonar sensors work much in the same way as LiDAR
sensors, only they send out sound waves. Sonar is
typically used underwater, because sound waves
can travel further underwater than light or radio
waves. Sonar is typically used to map the ocean
floor, search for underwater hazards, or locate
shipwrecks on the ocean floor.

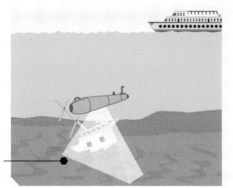

The sound waves are
reflected off a sunken ship.

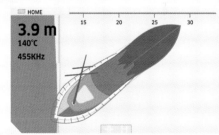

Sonar image
A sonar system produces an image of the
shipwreck, along with information on how
far away and how large it is.

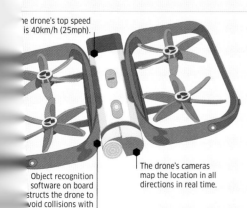

The drone's top speed
is 40km/h (25mph).

Object recognition
software on board
structs the drone to
void collisions with
s and other objects.

The drone's cameras
map the location in all
directions in real time.

SLAM

Simultaneous Localization and Mapping (SLAM) is
an exciting branch of robotic navigation that could
really aid future unmanned aerial vehicles (UAVs)
and land robots searching disaster sites for
survivors. SLAM calls for substantial computing
power to build and continually update a detailed
map of a robot's precise location and surroundings.
One autonomous drone, the Skydio R1, uses SLAM
and six pairs of navigation cameras to build a 3D
map of its local environment, avoid collisions, and
keep track of a moving object, which it films using
its video camera.

Tracking
The drone is able to track a target, such as this
person, even if the target makes sharp turns to
try to throw it off.

MANUFACTURER
NASA

ORIGIN
USA

DEVELOPED
2013

SPACE ROBOT

R5 VALKYRIE

The closest robotics has come to a modern-day superhero is NASA's photoshot humanoid robot R5 Valkyrie. This battery-powered bipedal robot can work alone in extreme environments without human assistance. Valkyrie is named after supernatural characters from Norse mythology who decided which warriors were rewarded in the afterlife. The robot builds on many years of NASA tests and feedback of previous robotic humanoids, and features numerous sensors and actuators (moving parts) designed to help it carry out complex tasks. Its next mission is to Mars, with Valkyrie expected to take its first steps on the Red Planet before human visitors.

The dark visor covers a 3D vision system and camera.

The bot's head can tilt and swivel around like a human head.

Each arm has seven joints and a group of actuators for motion.

The padded chest provides protection should the humanoid fall on its front.

MOON MACHINE

One of the robot world's latest lunar exploration rovers is *ATHLETE* (All-Terrain Hex-Legged Extra-Terrestrial Explorer). Like a futuristic, super-sized, six-limbed insect, this rover can walk or roll over bumpy Moon-like surfaces. Complete with a releasable grappling hook and a range of excavation instruments, *ATHLETE* is designed to move 100 times faster than existing exploration rovers.

HEIGHT
1.8 m (6.2 ft)

WEIGHT
136 kg (300 lb)

POWER
Battery

The limbs are removable and can be replaced quickly.

The plastic shell covering on the leg includes fans to keep the robot cool.

The bot's heavyset legs and wide feet ensure balance when the robot is walking.

The actuators in the bot's legs ensure easy movement.

The fabric-wrapped foam armour encases the robot's body for added protection.

"...robust, rugged, entirely electric humanoid robot capable of **operating in degraded... environments.**"

NASA

PREPPING FOR FUTURE

The Valkyrie team is constantly working to improve the bot's dexterity to enable it to work alongside astronauts in preparation for future exploration.

A series of tests have pushed Valkyrie to its limits. The robot can drive, climb a ladder, use power tools, and walk through unstable terrain without stumbling. This intensive preparation will prove beneficial when Valkyrie makes it to Mars.

Valkyrie's upgraded version includes modified humanoid hands to improve performance on the job. Each hand has three fingers and a thumb to grasp, manipulate, and work a variety of objects and instruments with precision and care. The actuators allow the wrists to roll easily, bringing further freedom of movement.

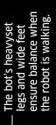

GLOSSARY

3D
An abbreviation of "three-dimensional", meaning something that creates the impression of depth, height, and length.

acceleration
A change in speed.

accelerometer
An instrument for measuring acceleration.

actuator
A moving part of a robot, such as a motor or a robot's arm.

aerodynamics
The study of how solid objects move through air.

algorithm
A series of steps taken by a computer to solve a problem or carry out a task.

android robot
A robot that is a convincing imitation of a living human being, rather than just a humanoid. Androids exist only in fiction at present.

application (app)
A piece of software designed to achieve a particular purpose.

artificial intelligence
The simulation of intelligence that is demonstrated by computer programs and machines.

automatic
A word for an action that happens by itself with little or no human control.

automaton
A machine that imitates the actions of a person or animal, but without having any intelligence. An automaton is only able to perform a set of predetermined movements. Plural: automata.

autonomous
A term for anything artificial that can make decisions and act upon them without human help or control.

AUV
An acronym for "autonomous underwater vehicle", a crewless robot submarine used for underwater exploration.

avatar
A representation of a human in a place where they are not physically present.

biomimetic robot
A robot that has a design inspired by some aspect of the natural world, such as plants or animals.

bionic
Having a body part or parts that are artificial.

bipedal robot
A robot that uses two legs to move.

central processing unit (CPU)
The part of a computer that controls most of its operations. Also known as the microprocessor.

cloud
A term used for specialized computers that provide services through the internet, such as storing files.

code
Instructions written in programming language that tell a computer to do something.

collaborative robot
A robot that is designed to work alongside humans. Collaborative robots normally need to have extremely high safety precautions so that they will not hurt the humans they work with. Also known as a cobot.

component
A part of something. In robots, parts such as a sensor or a touchscreen are called components.

computer
An electronic device that manipulates data.

computer chip
A set of electronic circuits on a small piece of semiconducting material, usually silicon. Also known as an integrated circuit.

console
A device that contains controls for a machine or robot.

data
Measurements or other basic information collected and stored by a robot or artificial intelligence as it operates. A computer uses data to decide what the robot should do.

debugging
The process of finding and fixing bugs (errors) in programs.

dexterity
A robot's skill in performing tasks, especially with its arms or end effectors.

domestic robot
A robot designed to work alongside people in their homes.

drone
A remotely controlled pilotless flying machine. Some drones are not true robots as they lack autonomy and usually only have a basic level of intelligence.

edible robot
A robot that can carry out a task within a human or animal after being swallowed, before its parts dissolve harmlessly. No fully edible robot has been developed yet.

end effector
A part connected to the end of a robot arm where a hand would be in humans. End effectors are designed to carry out specific tasks and as such, come in a variety of designs.

environment
The location and conditions that a robot or other machine works in.

exoskeleton
A hard external covering for the body. Many insects have exoskeletons, and some kinds of robots do, too.

facial recognition
The ability for a robot to remember human faces, or to be able to respond to human facial expressions.

flowchart
A diagram that describes a sequence. A flowchart can be used to explain to a human what a computer program is doing and how it arrives at its decisions.

GPS
An acronym for "global positioning system", a system for determining the position of something on the Earth's surface by comparing radio signals from several satellites. The time differences between the signals are used to work out the position of a GPS receiver to within a few metres.

gripper
A part of a robot that has the ability to hold and manipulate objects.

gyroscope
A device consisting of a wheel or disc mounted so that it can spin rapidly about an axis, which is itself free to alter in direction. The orientation of the axis is not affected by tilting, which makes a gyroscope a useful component in many machines to provide stability.

haptic
Relating to the sense of touch. A robot may give haptic feedback to a human in the form of vibrations or physical resistance.

hardware
The physical parts of a computer, such as the exterior casing and internal circuitry.

HD
An abbreviation of "high-definition". HD relates to the resolution (quality) of video, photograph, or sound data.

hexapod
A six-legged robot that displays a walking motion based on that of insects.

home assistant
A type of AI that is typically for the home and uses powerful microphones, special software, and an internet connection to respond to questions and instructions from its owner.

home-help robot
A robot that helps its user carry out tasks at home. Some home-help robots are designed to be used by disabled people.

humanoid robot
A robot with a face or body that is designed to be similar to that of a human. Humanoid robots usually have a head and arms, and sometimes legs.

hydraulic
Relating to the phenomenon of a liquid moving in a confined space under pressure. Hydraulics are used to cause parts to move in some robots.

industrial robot
A robot that works in a factory manufacturing things. Most are single arms that can move in several directions and can use a range of tools. Industrial robots make up the bulk of robots in use worldwide.

infrared
A kind of light that lies just beyond the red end of the visible light spectrum, invisible to the human eye. Some robots use it for navigation and communication.

interface
A device through which two different systems, or a human and a robot, can communicate. Remote controls and touchscreens are examples of interfaces.

internet
A massive global network created from connections between billions of computers.

joystick
A small lever used to control a machine.

laser
A device that emits a focussed beam of light. Sometimes the word is used to refer to the beam of light itself.

lateral
Referring to the side or sides of something. In movement, it means going sideways.

LED
An acronym for "light-emitting diode". A LED glows when a voltage is applied to it.

LiDAR
An acronym of "light-detection and ranging", a system that involves sending out beams of light and measuring the reflected light when it bounces off solid objects. Some robots use it to detect things in their environment.

longitudinal
Referring to something that runs lengthways as opposed to across.

machine
Something artificial that is powered by energy and is used to carry out a task.

MAV
An acronym for "micro aerial vehicle", a miniature UAV (umanned aerial vehicle).

mechanical
Operated by or relating to a machine or machines.

medical assistant robot
A robot that performs a task or tasks to help its disabled operator, and sometimes used to refer to robots that help in medical procedures.

microcontroller
A controlling device that includes a microprocessor.

microphone
A device that takes sound waves and turns them into a digital signal that can then be amplified, transmitted, or recorded.

microprocessor
The part of a computer that controls most of its operations. Also known as the CPU.

module
A self-contained section of a robot or a computer program. Modules can be designed and tested separately, and then joined to form the finished product.

monitor
A screen that is used to display computer information.

motherboard
The place where various parts of a computer connect. The motherboard houses the CPU, memory, and other parts, and is where sensors connect.

motor
A device that changes electricity into movement. Motors are used to make robots move.

nanorobot
A robot so small it is only visible under a microscope. No nanorobots have yet been made, but possible techniques for making them are being explored.

navigation
The process of a human or robot accurately figuring out where they are, and planning and following a route.

network
A group of connected devices that can share resources and data. Networks can be classified by size or topology (layout).

neural network
An artificial brain made by connecting large numbers of electronic nerve cells, often simulated on a computer. Neural networks can do difficult jobs, like recognizing faces.

OS
An acronym for "operating system", a piece of software that manages a computer's hardware and software resources, and makes it easier for them to be used.

piezoelectric
Something that produces an electric charge when put under stress.

piloted robot
A robot that is controlled wholly or in part by a human. Piloted robots are not true robots as they do not have a reasonable level of autonomy.

pneumatic
Relating to the phenomenon of air moving in a confined space under pressure. Pneumatics are used to cause parts to move in some robots.

portable
A term for something that is easy to carry or move around.

program
A collection of instructions that performs a specific task when executed by a computer.

programming
The process of giving instructions to a computer.

programming language
A formalized set of words and symbols that allows a person to give instructions to a computer.

propeller
A mechanical device that is used to drive something forward. A propeller consists of a central revolving shaft with two or more broad, angled blades attached to it.

prosthetic
An artificial body part that replaces one that is missing, such as a leg or hand.

proximity sensor
A sensor that is designed to measure very small distances between a robot and an object.

radar
An acronym for "radio detection and ranging", a system that involves sending out radio waves and measuring the reflected radio waves when they bounce off solid objects. Some robots use it to detect things in their environment.

robot
A moving machine that is programmed by a computer to do different tasks. Most robots can sense their environment, and have some ability to respond to it autonomously.

robot arm
A versatile, computer-controlled, jointed arm that can handle tools and do factory work. It is the most common type of robot in use.

roboticist
A scientist or engineer who specializes in making or studying robots.

rotor
A part of a machine that turns around a central axis. Rotors are primarily used to provide lift in aircraft, but are also used in gyroscopes.

rover
A robot designed to roam around, typically on a remote planet, to survey the landscape, take samples, and make measurements.

sensor
A component of a robot or machine that picks up information from its surroundings, such as eyes or a camera. There are many types of sensor.

simulation
A computer model of something. Robot simulations help operators understand how the instructions they want to give a robot will likely be understood and executed by the robot, in a safe environment.

snakebot
A type of robot that features a long, flexible, slender body that looks and moves much like a snake.

social robot
A robot that is designed to interact and converse with humans.

soft robot
A robot made using soft, pliable materials as opposed to hard, rigid ones.

software
The operating system, programs, and firmware that allows a user to access a computer's hardware.

sonar
An acronym for "sound navigation and ranging", a system that involves sending out sound waves and measuring the reflected sound waves when they bounce off solid objects. Some robots use it to detect things in their environment.

space robot
A robot that is designed to explore planets, moons, and other things beyond Earth.

stereo camera
A camera with two or more lenses, or two or more cameras that work in tandem, with the aim of creating an effect similar to a human's stereoscopic vision.

stimulus
A thing or event that causes a reaction in something. Plural: stimuli.

submersible
A craft that is designed to operate underwater.

swarm robot
A small robot that has its own intelligence and can act autonomously, but also as part of a large group of similar robots.

tablet computer
A type of portable computer that accepts input primarily via a touchscreen, and outputs information mainly through apps (applications).

tactile
Relating to the sense of touch. A robot may give tactile feedback to a human in the form of vibrations or physical resistance.

teaching pendant
A digital device that is used to instruct or program a robot to do a task. It is usually tethered to the robot in some way.

thruster
A small rocket engine on a spacecraft, or a secondary jet or propeller on a ship or underwater craft, used to make small alterations to the craft's position or route.

transducer
A device that converts variations in a physical quantity, such as pressure or brightness, into an electrical signal, or vice versa.

transistor
A tiny device that is used to amplify or switch electric current. Transistors are the building blocks of computer chips.

transmitter
Something that generates and sends a signal.

tread
The thick part of a robot's wheel that grips the ground or any other surface.

trilateration
The method of determining location that a GPS device uses. It involves the GPS device receiving location and time data from three GPS satellites and then using the information to pinpoint exactly where it is.

Turing test
A blind test outlined by English mathematician Alan Turing that centres on the ability for an evaluator to assess whether any particular machine can be said to be intelligent.

UAV
An acronym for "unmanned aerial vehicle", an aircraft piloted by remote control or on-board computers.

wireless
A type of technology whereby data is sent to or from a machine or robot without the use of a physical connection.

work robot
A robot primarily designed to carry out tasks for humans.

INDEX

ACKNOWLEDGMENTS

Dorling Kindersley would like to thank the following people for their assistance with their book: Tony Prescott, Michael Szollosy, Jonathan Aiken, Daniel Camilleri, Michael Port, Giovanni Reina, Salah Talamali, and Natalie Wood from the robotics laboratory in the University of Sheffield, UK; Priyanka Kharbanda, Smita Mathur, Sophie Parkes, Neha Ruth Samuel, and Vatsal Verma for editorial assistance; Mansi Agarwal, Priyanka Bansal, Kanupriya Lal, Arun Pottirayil, and Heena Sharma for making illustrations; Katie John for proofreading; and Helen Peters for indexing.

Picture Credits

The publisher would like to thanks the following for their kind permission to reproduce their photographs:

(Key: a–above; b–below/bottom; c–centre; f–far; l–left; r–right; t–top)

1 The Ripper Group International: (c). 2-3 © Engineered Arts Limited: (c). 4 Alamy Stock Photo: Aflo Co. Ltd. (br). 5 Dorling Kindersley. Marsi Bionics. 6 Dorling Kindersley. Festo. 7 Dorling Kindersley. NASA: JSC (bl). 8 Dorling Kindersley. 10-11 Alamy Stock Photo: dpa picture alliance (c). 12 Alamy Stock Photo: Chronicle (bl); ZUMA Press, Inc (bc). Dorling Kindersley. Getty Images: baranozdemir (br). 13 Dorling Kindersley. Rex by Shutterstock: Tony Kyriacou (bl). 14 Rex by Shutterstock: Carnegie Mellon University (tr). Rotundus AB: (cr). 14-15 Festo. 15 Dorling Kindersley. Getty Images: Monty Rakusen (tl). NASA: JPL (cr). 16 Alamy Stock Photo: Malcolm Park editorial (bl). Rex by Shutterstock: Cardiff Univeristy / Epa (cl). 16-17 Alamy Stock Photo: World History Archive (tc). 17 123RF.com: tomas1111 (bc). Alamy Stock Photo: North Wind Picture Archives (bl). 18 akg-images: Eric Lessing (tl). Alamy Stock Photo: INTERFOTO (bl). 18-19 Rex by Shutterstock: Everett Kennedy Brown / EPA (c). 19 akg-images: (tr). Alamy Stock Photo: Granger Historical Picture Archive (cr). 20-21 Getty Images: Bettmann (bc). 20 Alamy Stock Photo: Art Collection 3 (tc). Getty Images: Historical (cl); Science and Society Picture Library (c). 21 Alamy Stock Photo: Granger Historical Picture Archive (tr). Getty Images: Andrew Burton (tl). 22-23 Alamy Stock Photo: Paramountn Pictures (c). 22 Alamy Stock Photo: Chronicle (tl); World History Archive (cl). Rex by

Shutterstock: Universal History Archive / Universal Images Group (tc). 23 Alamy Stock Photo: AF Archive (br); Everett Collection Inc (cr). Dreamstime.com: Mark Eaton (tr). 24-25 Alamy Stock Photo: Aflo Co. Ltd. (bc). 24 123RF.com: Alexander Kolomietz (bl). Getty Images: The Washington Post (tl). 25 Dorling Kindersley: Richard Leeney (bc/ball). Marsi Bionics: (cr). Rimac Automobili: (tl). 26 ABB Ltd.. Dorling Kindersley. Leka: (cl). NASA: JPL (bl). 27 ASUS: (cr). Dorling Kindersley. Festo. Getty Images: David Hecker (tl); Chip Somodevilla (tr). Marsi Bionics. 28 ASUS. 29 ASUS. 30-31 Dorling Kindersley. 32-33 Courtesy of Boston Dynamics. 32 Courtesy of Boston Dynamics. 33 Courtesy of Boston Dynamics. 36-37 Marsi Bionics. 36 ReWalk Robotics GmbH: (bl). 37 Marsi Bionics: (tc). 38 Dorling Kindersley: Dreamstime.com / Prykhodov (tl). 38-39 ASUS. 39 Dorling Kindersley. 40 iRobot: (cr). The Kobi Company: (tl). Pillo Inc: (bl). 41 iRobot. 42-43 HOOBOX Robotics: (all photos). 44-45 Anki. 44 Anki. 45 Anki. 48-49 Leka: (all photos apart from tablet at bottom left). 48 Dorling Kindersley. 50-51 Dorling Kindersley. 52 Dorling Kindersley. 52-53 Dorling Kindersley. 53 Getty Images: Bloomberg (bl). 54-55 Dorling Kindersley. 58-59 Getty Images: 3alexd (c). 58 Intuitive Surgical, Inc.. 59 Intuitive Surgical, Inc.: (br). 60 Cobalt Robotics: Gustav Rehnby (cl, bl). OC Robotics: (cr). 60-61 Stanley Robotics: (tc). 61 iRobot. Rotundus AB. Simbe Robotics Inc: (cl). 64-65 Dorling Kindersley: (all photos). 66-67 Dorling Kindersley. 68-69 Dorling Kindersley. 70-71 Dorling Kindersley. 72-73 Piaggio Fast Forward: (all photos). 76-77 Dorling Kindersley. 76 Dorling Kindersley. Getty Images: David Hecker (tl). 78-79 Dorling Kindersley. 80-81 Matthew Shave for Stylist Magazine: (c). 81 Rex by Shutterstock: Ken McKay / ITV (crb). Matthew Shave for Stylist Magazine. 82 © Engineered Arts Limited: (bl). Swisslog Healthcare: (tl). Waseda University., Tokyo, Japan: Atsuo Takanishi Lab. (c). 83 Compressorhead: (tl). Rex by Shutterstock: Aflo (c, br). Toyota (GB) PLC: (bl). 84-85 ABB Ltd.: (c). 84 Getty Images: AFP (bl). 85 Getty Images: Haruyoshi Yamaguchi / Bloombert (br). 86-87 Moley Robotics: (all photos). 88-89 Dorling Kindersley. 90 Dorling Kindersley. 90-91 Dorling Kindersley. 91 Getty Images: BSIP / Universal Images Group (tc). 92-93 Dorling Kindersley. 94-95 MegaBots, Inc: (c). 94 MegaBots, Inc. 96 Dorling Kindersley. 96-97 Dorling Kindersley.

97 AIST: (tr). Rex by Shutterstock: APA-PictureDesk GmbH (br). 98-99 Festo. 100-101 Faraday Future. 100 Faraday Future. 101 Faraday Future. 102-103 Festo. 104-105 Teddy Seguin: © Osada / Seguin / DRASSM (c/main robot image). 105 Teddy Seguin: © Osada / Seguin / DRASSM (br). 108-109 Festo. 109 Festo. 110-111 Festo: (c). 112-113 Harvard John A. Paulson School of Engineering and Applied Sciences: (all photos). 114 Courtesy of Boston Dynamics: (cl). Johns Hopkins University Applied Physics Laboratory: (br). SRI International: (tr). 115 National Oceanography Centre, Southampton: (tc). RSE:RobotsISE.org. Stanford News Service. : Linda A. Cicero (br). 116-117 Festo: (all photos). 120-121 Eelume AS: (all photos). 122-123 Eelume AS. 124-125 Festo. 128 Harvard John A. Paulson School of Engineering and Applied Sciences. 128-129 Harvard John A. Paulson School of Engineering and Applied Sciences. 129 Harvard John A. Paulson School of Engineering and Applied Sciences. 130-131 NASA: JSC (c). 132-133 NASA: JPL (c). 133 NASA: JPL (c). 136-137 The Ripper Group International: (c). 136 The Ripper Group International. 138-139 HANKOOK MIRAE TECHNOLOGY, www.k-technology.co.kr. 138 Getty Images: Chung Sung-Jun (ca). HANKOOK MIRAE TECHNOLOGY, www.k-technology.co.kr: (tl). 140 Lockheed Martin: (tr). Massachusetts Institute of Technology (MIT): Underworlds is a project by the MIT Senseable CIty Lab and Alm Lab (cl, c, bc). USC Institute for Creative Technologies: (br). 141 Farshad Arvin: (bc). DVIDS: Sgt Cody Quinn (tr). 142-143 Sarcos: (all photos). 144-145 Carnegie Mellon University. 146-147 Carnegie Mellon University: (c). 150-151 NASA: JSC (c). 150 NASA: JPL (br)

All other images © Dorling Kindersley
For further information see:
www.dkimages.com